THE WAY

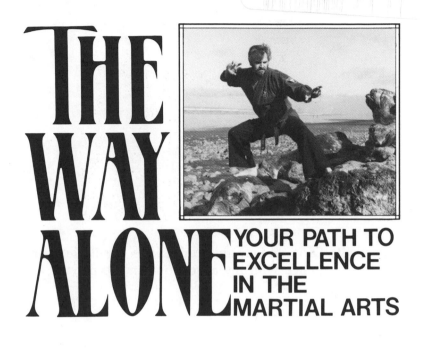

ALONE

YOUR PATH TO EXCELLENCE IN THE MARTIAL ARTS

To my wife, Lana, and my children, Carrie, Daniel, and Amy, for their patience with my absorption in the martial arts.

THE WAY ALONE

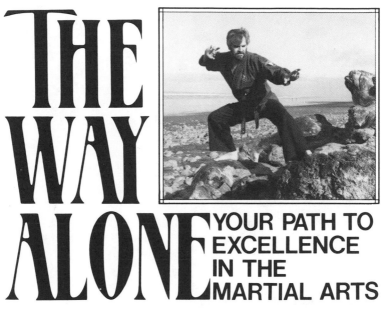

YOUR PATH TO EXCELLENCE IN THE MARTIAL ARTS

PALADIN PRESS
BOULDER, COLORADO

The Way Alone
Your Path to Excellence in the Martial Arts
by Loren W. Christensen
Copyright © 1987 by Loren W. Christensen

ISBN 0-87364-421-2
Printed in the United States of America

Published by Paladin Press, a division of
Paladin Enterprises, Inc., P.O. Box 1307,
Boulder, Colorado 80306, USA.
(303) 443-7250

Direct inquiries and/or orders to the above address.

Neither the author nor the publisher assumes
any responsibility for the use or misuse of
information contained in this book.

Also by Loren Christensen:

Anything Goes: Practical Karate for the Streets

The Way of the Warrior: The Violent Side

Winning with American Kata: The New Breed of Competitors

Contents

Foreword   vii

Preface   ix

About the Author   xiii

Chapter 1
Mental Training   1

Chapter 2
Reps   19

Chapter 3
Environmental Training   53

Chapter 4
Kata   73

Chapter 5
Cardiovascular Training   79

Chapter 6
Weight Training   89

Chapter 7
Bag Work   99

Chapter 8
The Final Punch   107

Acknowledgments

I'd like to thank all my instructors for pointing the way: Bruce Terrill, karate; Leonard Trigg, arnis, t'ai chi, and kung fu; Remy Presas, arnis; Rick Alamany, karate and jujutsu; and Jim Pearson, t'ai chi.

A very special thanks to my friend Renardo Barden, for editing this text and sharing his experience and knowledge of the art and business of writing.

Thanks to Lana, Gary Sussman, and Anna McAllister for their time spent behind the camera.

Foreword

When I first started my training in karate, there were very few books written on the subject. The few that were in print dealt with the basic stances, punches, blocks, and kicks. The type of book you are about to read hadn't been written nor has the subject of training alone been thoroughly covered in the twenty years since I began training.

Loren W. Christensen was my first instructor. I studied under Loren from 1966 through 1967, until he went into the army. Those first months were to shape everything I was to become later in the martial arts. I recall hard, hard workouts in which Loren was right there, sweating along with the rest of the class. As hard as we trained, I always had the feeling that he was putting more intensity into each punch than anyone else in the class. It was that intensity that I tried to put into my workouts after he left.

I was fourteen years old when I started with Loren and I immediately became consumed with training, in class and on my own. I was what you would call a "karate nut" and I decided then to make karate my sole endeavor, the thing I would use to make my niche in the world.

When you are smitten by the martial arts, you are willing to put in extra time to train. But when you want to put in an extra workout on your own, you may immediately be faced with the question: "What can I do?"

This book answers that question and in doing so fills a void in karate training that has never been dealt with by the hundreds of martial arts books on the market today. The key ingredient to putting together a solo workout is to make it interesting. Loren fills this book with a wide variety of solo drills that are not only productive but are interesting to do. This book will get you sparked and revved up to work out. *The Way Alone* will be a valuable aid to your training.

Dan Anderson
American Freestyle
Portland, Oregon

Preface

There wasn't a book like this when I started karate in the hot summer of 1965. In fact, I don't think there were more than half a dozen karate books in existence back then. Nor could the few people involved in karate then have imagined that it would grow and develop into what it has become today.

In the beginning, I attended classes two or three times a week at the Oregon Karate Association under the guidance of Bruce Terrill. From the very start, I was hooked and found great joy in the line drills, sparring, and kata. It gave rise to a strange energy and joy, this punching and kicking, and I can still remember the sound of thirty gi popping simultaneously as we kicked and punched, how the floor shook when stomped by sixty feet, and the way the walls reverberated with our shouts.

But as much as I enjoyed training with my fellow students, I soon discovered that I also liked training alone—maybe even more so. In school, I never cared for team sports, nor was I interested in competition—at least in the sense of trying to be better than someone else. However, even as a kid I sought out activities where I could compete against myself, setting new goals to reach, and finding new obstacles to overcome.

I soon found that the martial arts fulfilled this part of my personality that craved a physical outlet. Then when I discovered the added joys of solo training, it was like topping the pudding with a cherry. I could acquire the new karate knowledge and, when alone, apply the techniques and concepts to my need for goal setting, self-discipline, self-competition, and creative expression.

After about a month of training, Mr. Terrill taught my class the side kick. Although I understood the mechanics of the movement, I just couldn't get my body to cooperate. The difference between Mr. Terrill's side kick and my own was like the difference between the graceful cantering movements of a beautiful show horse and those of a newborn pony struggling to stay up on its wobbly legs. Frustrated, but with a new goal in mind, I went home that Friday determined to bring my brain and body together before my next class on Monday.

For the next two days and nights, I trained on that side kick with a fanaticism that bordered on obsession. First I broke the kick down into several movements: lifting the leg, sliding it up, cocking the kick, hand placement, supporting leg placement, hip rotation, thrusting the kick out, retracting the leg, and snapping it down to its original position. To develop correct form, I watched my image in the hall mirror, my shadow on the side of the house, and at night, my reflection in the living room window.

I experimented with kicking on different foundations, such as the waxed kitchen floor, the rough driveway cement, the early-morning wet grass, and the soft, plowed earth of a vegetable garden. I kicked repetition after repetition while continuing to analyze my own form, correct my errors, and target the kick where I wanted it to travel.

Finally, tired and sore, my enthusiasm began to wane. But I still wasn't ready to give up. I turned on the stereo and began kicking to the pronounced beat of a Beatles record. To my surprise, a new surge of energy and rhythm began flowing into my movements. Late at night I listened to mellow jazz and practiced in total darkness in order to develop a kinesthetic feel for correct technique. Mornings I trained in a nearby park, exhilarated by the sunshine's warm, golden rays cascading down on me through a canopy of pine needles.

By Sunday my muscles and even my bones hurt, but I had the correct form. It looked good and it felt good. Oh, there were still rough edges, and I had a long way to go to obtain power, speed, and the skill of application, but all my solo work had done the integrating trick. In just two days my side kick had improved 100 percent.

Obviously, you can't reach all your martial arts goals in a single weekend. But this early solo-training experience stayed with me. I learned that privately I could supplement and improve what I learned in class, and I could do it on my own time and in my own place.

Since that experience twenty-one years ago, I'd estimate that two-thirds of my training has been solo. I can't recall ever being bored working out alone, because I have always used my mind to plan and create new methods and goals for myself. The years of solo training have provided me with many fond memories.

I can recall performing kata in a ninety-mile-an-hour hurricane in the Florida Keys, and practicing the soft, flowing movements of t'ai chi while the orange sun set off the California coast. While in the army I lived for a time in a room that measured eight feet by eight feet. My training there gave me an appreciation for the dynamics of fighting in a crowded space. For several months I trained in a hot Texas desert with only cactus and lizards for company. There were many humid nights in Vietnam when I trained by punching tree trunks and kicking branches, while the sounds of war pounded in the distance. I have a fond memory of walking alone in the rich green hills of Kyoto, Japan, where samurai, Ninja, and the old masters had trained, fought, and died. Kata training there was for me not so much physical as profoundly spiritual. Perhaps, I mused, some of what had gone on before me would be absorbed by my own perspiring body.

Solo training has been invaluable to me. I have used it to develop strength, speed, explosiveness, endurance, timing, discipline, stress reduction, and other qualities. Even today, I supplement my own group training and teaching schedule with solo workouts three times weekly.

Over the years I've heard students express the viewpoint that they hate training alone: "I don't like to train by myself; it's so boring. I don't know what to do." This book, then, represents solo training methods I have used and taught my students to use since 1965. They all work and may be either used on an "as is" basis or modified in countless ways to help you reach your own personal training goals.

While I recognize there are those who live a great distance from a martial arts school, I am certainly not advocating that you try to learn the martial arts by yourself. You definitely need instruction from a qualified teacher, as well as relationships with other students and different opponents on whom you can try your techniques safely. More than anything else, this solo-training book is intended to help you get acquainted with the very definite pleasures and benefits of training by yourself. . .after you've trained with others.

Karate is more than fighting. It is a road to self-discovery. I can think of no better way to test your discipline, strengthen your fortitude, and coordinate your mind and body than to practice training solo. Walk the path alone and I guarantee you'll begin to discover many things never seen by those who only train to the commanding voices of their instructors.

About the Author

Recognized today as a teacher and prolific writer of the martial arts, author Loren W. Christensen began his study of karate as a teenager under Bruce Terrill, founder of the Oregon Karate Association. Since 1965, Christensen's relentless study and search has taken him to many schools and teachers throughout the United States, Vietnam, and Japan in search of knowledge from all martial arts.

Over the years, Christensen has earned advanced black-belt ranking from the Oregon Karate Association and the American Teachers Association of the Martial Arts. He has also earned a black belt in arnis from the founder of modern arnis, Professor Remy Presas. Christensen is presently studying jujutsu.

As a police officer in Portland, Oregon, Christensen is a recognized authority on police defensive tactics, having taught and written extensively on the subject for many years. His first book, *An Introduction to Defensive Tactics for Law Enforcement Officers,* has been used by a variety of police agencies across the country. He is frequently called upon by the courts as an expert witness in cases involving the use of martial arts, martial arts weapons, and accusations of police excessive force.

Loren W. Christensen

Although his roots are in a tournament-oriented system, Christensen's pursuit of knowledge has always been for techniques that are practical and realistic for the street. In the early years, Christensen was a tournament fighter but because of harsh experiences as a military policeman in Vietnam and as a street officer in Portland, his interests were directed toward the martial arts' original precepts of self-defense rather than sport. By contrast, however, he enjoys the artistic elements of karate and practices kata for physical, mental, and spiritual growth. He competes in kata and weapons and has been rated by *Karate Illustrated* magazine as a top-ten form competitor in Region I, the states of Oregon, Washington, Idaho, Wyoming, and Montana.

Today Christensen teaches an eclectic style which combines the best techniques from karate, kung fu, jujutsu, and arnis. His classes and writings, however, teach much more than just the physical elements of fighting. He believes the secret to success in defeating an attacker on the street or an opponent in the ring, or in bringing out a student's maximum potential, lies within the mind. And that belief is echoed in this book.

Chapter 1
Mental Training

Visualization is a process of using mental imagery to help develop physical skill, improve self-image, reach goals, and prepare for high-risk situations. The process is not a mystical oriental concept with deep roots in Zen Buddhism or Confucianism. Visualization is a relatively simple training method that emphasizes attaining physical and mental goals within short periods of time.

Most of us are already familiar with the negative side of visualization: "I've never really been any good at tournament sparring. I practice karate mainly to stay in shape and to meet new friends. I love karate, but my sparring never improves. I'd like to be better at it, but I guess I never will be. I don't think well in a tournament situation; I get really nervous and I don't know what to do. Maybe I'm just not a tournament fighter."

This is a psychological self-portrait of a karate student named Cindy. Like her, all of us carry around a mental picture of ourselves based on accumulated past experiences. The problem is that once we have developed the self-portrait, we tend to believe it. And if our portrait is negative, like Cindy's, it becomes an obstacle to future improvement.

Because of Cindy's past experiences at sparring, specifically tournament sparring, she has developed the notion that she is not a competitor and can't become one. This mental image has become so clear to her that it dictates how she thinks, behaves, and performs physically. When she thinks, "my sparring will not improve," it won't. When she believes, "I don't think well in a tournament situation," her actions confirm her belief. When she sums it all up by saying, "maybe I'm just not a tournament fighter," she never will be. As long as she pictures herself as a loser, she always will be one. Until she reconstructs her self-portrait, her performance will reflect her negative beliefs 90 percent of the time; she will not improve.

To reconstruct her self-portrait, she must develop an image that is positive toward tournament competition. She must think, act, and practice as if she were already a winner. She must convince herself that she is a tournament fighter who can fight with courage and intelligence and that she will continue to improve day after day. With this positive image completely embedded in her conscious and subconscious mind, all her actions will combine to reinforce her new self-image.

Creating a Better Self-Image

Creating a better self-image will enable you to release and use abilities that you may not have known you even possessed. Once you realize your skills are improving, your self-image will continue to become more positive. It's like a circle: a more positive self-image improves your skill, and that improved skill base improves your self-image.

Cindy's negative self-image is a product of a negative video cassette tape that has been playing in her brain. This tape has been continually projecting an image that she has been mimicking. Her goal then, is to erase the tape, create a positive one, and get on the path to a better self-image and greater progress in the martial arts.

Your goal should be the same. Once you have decided upon

Your mind is more receptive to creating positive tapes when you have achieved a relaxed state through meditation and proper breathing.

a realistic self-image, you are ready to begin imprinting a new picture in your mind. You will find that your mind is

Meditation and visualization can be
practiced in a quiet room or anywhere
that is serene.

most receptive when you are in a relaxed state.

Step one: relax. One technique for achieving relaxation is to first set aside about ten minutes, twice each day, in a quiet place where you will not be disturbed. If you have a busy schedule, you can use this method before getting out of bed in the morning and before going to sleep at night. Lie comfortably, close your eyes, and begin breathing slowly and deeply through your nostrils. Draw the air deeply into your lower abdomen and hold it for a moment before you slowly exhale through your slightly parted lips.

As your inhale, visualize the oxygen as a pale blue fog that is swirling into your chest, stomach, legs, and arms. Feel this cool fog relax you and draw all the stress and tension from your body. As your hold your breath for a moment, see the fog quickly change to red as it mixes with these unwanted properties. Exhale and envision the hot, red fog flowing from your arms, legs, chest, and stomach, leaving you relaxed and sinking deeper into your mattress. Repeat this cycle several times until you are thoroughly relaxed.

Yet another method of relaxing entails lying or sitting comfortably and breathing very slowly. Envision yourself descending a flight of stairs. Tell yourself that with each step down you are becoming more and more relaxed. Continue to descend the steps until you are completely relaxed. But don't fall asleep!

Once you feel relaxed, imagine yourself at a table on which there are several bottles and a drinking glass. The bottles contain all of the characteristics that you want to possess. There are bottles of confidence, courage, a winning attitude, self-discipline, and whatever else you lack. Mentally mix all of the contents of these bottles into the glass and drink. As the beverage enters your body, feel it flow into your limbs and into your mind. Feel the mixture completely saturating your tissues and forming a new you.

After you have finished your drink, mentally stand in front of a full-length mirror and see and feel it as all of these new qualities revitalize and electrify you into the person you want to be. Feel this new power straighten your back, pull your shoulders back, expand your chest, and charge your muscles with surging energy. Look at yourself and believe that you are now that person and you can perform as you want.

Brimming with this new high-powered attitude, you will now see yourself as a new martial artist. Picture yourself putting on your gi as if you were Clark Kent stripping off his business suit and donning his brilliant red and blue tights and cape. Now you're ready for battle. See yourself walk—swagger if you want—to the center of the dojo floor ready for anything your teacher gives you. Bow with confidence to your imaginary opponent and snap into your fighting stance, ready to unleash your fury on your poor, unsuspecting sparring partner. No matter how or where you visualize yourself, you are always overflowing with confidence and the knowledge that you are good and getting better. You are growing stronger, faster, and more skillful each day. In other words, *you are a winner!*

Imagine that all of the characteristics in the drink are now permanently part of you. Say to yourself, "I will let go of any thoughts that will hold me back. I will let go of any mental tapes that prevent me from being all that I can be."

You are now ready to return to the regular world. Count from one to five and feel yourself returning to your surroundings. Open your eyes, take a few deep breaths, and feel the new positive energy as it flows through your body.

As mentioned, this approach to developing an improved self-image is best performed in a quiet and relaxed state. Practice it twice a day for three weeks and you will be amazed at your improvements. It takes little effort considering that you have probably spent a good portion of your life developing your negative tape.

Affirmative Visualization

Webster's New World Dictionary, Second College Edition, defines *affirm* as "to say positively; declare firmly; assert to be true...to make valid...confirm."

The use of positive self-affirmation is a method of mentally using phrases to create a better self-image as well as improve physical technique. Negative affirmation statements, such as "I'll never have a good back kick," or "I won't do well in the tournament," will be your belief system if you repeat them often enough. You need to eliminate such thoughts and replace them with positive phrases.

Choose phrases that are short, positive, and to the point: "I will do well in the tournament. I am a winner. I will act like a winner. I will fight like a winner. This tournament is good for me. It will make me stronger."

Use these phrases or create your own, and repeat them throughout the day. Although you can repeat the phrases out loud while you are driving, walking, or training, remember that your subconscious mind is most receptive while you are in a relaxed meditative state. Additionally, it is more effective to form a mental picture to coincide with the phrase. For example, when you say, "I am a winner," see yourself walking, talking, and performing as a winner. The combining of visualization and affirmation will accelerate you toward your goal.

The first step in improving karate technique is to get rid of such negatives as "I'll never have a good back kick." Monitor these thoughts and immediately replace any negative ones with: "My back kick is getting better. My back kick is getting faster. With every repetition my back kick gets stronger." Repeat these phrases often, especially while you are practicing the kick.

Definitely do not put yourself down. Learn to accept compliments. If someone says you performed a nice kata or that you have beautiful technique, do not reject the compliment in an attempt to be humble. Instead, thank them and explain that that is your favorite technique or that you enjoy performing that kata. Although we are taught to be humble in our art, the refusal of compliments by putting yourself down reinforces your negative self-image.

Improving Technique with Visualization

A unique study was conducted in which some basketball players were separated into three groups. Group A was instructed to practice shooting baskets for one hour every day from the free-throw line. Group B was told only to visualize the process for one hour every day, mentally seeing themselves with the ball, shooting with flawless form, and watching the ball swoosh through the hoop. Group C, the control group, was instructed not to spend any extra time shooting from the free-throw line.

After several weeks passed, the three groups were tested. It was discovered that Group C, the control group, did not improve at all. Group A made the most progress, but surprisingly, Group B, the group limited to mental practice, improved nearly to the same level as Group A.

Other studies conducted on a variety of skills reported similar results. The group limited to visualizing its practice was either comparable or nearly comparable to the group that physically practiced.

Visualization ought to be an important addition to your regular physical practice. Every time you practice visualizing a single technique, combination, or kata, you increase the possibility that your performance, in reality, will improve too. For example, say that on Friday your karate instructor teaches you a combination backfist fake, roundhouse kick to the groin, and straight punch to the abdomen. Not a difficult combination, but one which nevertheless requires coordination, balance, timing, and speed.

The instructor breaks it down into three or four steps, and you practice it in the air. Toward the end of the class he has you try it with a partner; however, there is just enough time left to do it three or four times. As the instructor bows out the class, he says you will continue to work on the combination the following Monday.

You've just been presented with an excellent opportunity for visualization practice.

Upon waking Saturday morning, you can practice your new combination before getting out of bed while you are calm, relaxed, and more receptive to the mental imagery. Strive for the utmost clarity in your mind as you go through the combination. See your lead hand whip out a backfist, your footwork as you slide up and launch a low roundhouse kick, and your follow-up punch to the stomach. Keep looking until your picture becomes as clear as the image on a television screen and each aspect of the combination comes in with razor sharpness.

Visualize the technique throughout the day, whether you are in your car, sitting on your sofa, or eating lunch. You can even add to the movements by seeing an opponent respond to the combination. See him trying to block the backfist, dropping his guard too late to block the roundhouse, and becoming wide open to receive your punch. Imagine him reacting in a variety of ways, even to the point of successfully blocking or evading your first two moves. You will then have to visualize the necessary adjustments in your technique until you can hit him with at least the last technique. It is important that no matter how elaborate the scenario, you must win; you must be successful at getting the point.

Visualize it all again that night in bed after you have induced a relaxed state of mind. Do it as many times as you can, allowing yourself to fall asleep in the process.

Repeat on Sunday. The more times you can go through the combination, the more entrenched it will be in your mind and body. As with any physical skill, the more you practice, the better you will become. Although it may at first seem otherwise, not that much time is involved. All it takes is ten minutes in the morning, ten minutes in the evening, and a few minutes two or three times during the day.

Back at the dojo on Monday, you and your instructor will be amazed at your improvement. Why? Because for the last two days you will have "practiced" the combination dozens of times. With the natural relationship between mind and body, your body will perform, not knowing or even caring that your last two days of practice were conducted only in your head.

Tournament Competition—Forms

On the day of the tournament, use your commuting time to visualize the kata competition. Begin by playing those positive affirmation tapes that confirm that you are ready, willing, and able to get out there and show what you can do. Feel the anticipation tingle through your limbs and think of those butterflies in your stomach as a positive energy that will give you strength.

Visualize your performance with great clarity and even emotional involvement. If music helps, listen to your favorite radio station or put in a cassette tape that is inspirational. Hear your name called and see yourself walk confidently up to the judges, bow, and boldly announce your name and the name of your kata.

Feel yourself pause for a moment as your fighting spirit builds and threatens to spill like an over-burdened dam. When the moment is right—*wham!*—explode into your first movement, visualizing not only the image, but feeling the power, speed, and intent. Proceed mentally through the entire form and finish with spirit and the confidence that comes from knowing you have performed an excellent form, *a winning form.*

After you have arrived at the tournament and have greeted your classmates and friends, find a quiet spot where you can continue your visualizing. If there is a movement that has been causing you problems, perform it correctly in your mind over and over. Do not let the incorrect method enter your mind but see only the correct technique performed with clarity and precision.

After you stretch out and have performed a warm-up kata, you will feel as if you have already practiced it several times. When you go out to compete, your body will be performing closely to your mental and physical practice. Also, by having seen yourself as confident, powerful, and precise, you will have become that which you have grown to believe, and as a result, you will perform in a like manner.

Tournament Competition—Fighting

If you are competing in fighting, visualization will work just as well. Picture yourself as confident, strong, fast, and responsive to any type of attack. Erase all negative tapes and see yourself with all the characteristics that will make you a winner.

Picture yourself bowing to the referee and your opponent. Assume your fighting stance and begin to stalk your opponent with enough determination to humble a tiger. See his lead hand drop and your responding backfist explode into the open target. He throws a roundhouse kick, but you easily block it and counter with a hard punch to his midsection.

If you know that you will be fighting a specific opponent, visualize his favorite attacks. See that punch of his, block it easily, and then counter with the match-winning point. Analyze the weaknesses in his personal style of fighting and imagine yourself taking advantage with scoring techniques. Feel your confidence and see yourself winning. *Always see yourself winning.*

Visualizing High-Risk Situations

You can also use visualization to take the fear out of high-risk situations that require quick thinking. Any thought-out plan of action that is developed before an actual situation unfolds is better than no plan—even if your plan isn't perfect. The practice of visualization will take the newness out of an event and make it possible for you to respond with a level of experience.

By training in mental imagery, you will have already faced the high-risk situation, or at least one that is similar. Your mental practice will help alleviate the hesitation caused by wondering what to do in a critical situation and will help you to avoid the mistakes that can occur when making decisions in a split second. Since, mentally at least, you have been in a similar situation before, your decision-making skills will be more fluid and accurate.

For example, you are walking at night to the bus stop when suddenly an unsavory type with assault and robbery on his mind steps out from a dark doorway. Oftentimes such a situation is so frightening that the victim will be frozen with fear and unable to think clearly or react properly. This is because the victim has been taken by surprise and is therefore forced to try to think under extremely stressful conditions.

By having practiced visualization, you will be one step ahead. Although a person suddenly stepping out from the shadows may still frighten you, you will be less taken aback by the confrontation because you have previously visualized, in detail, a number of similar situations. You will be more likely to act rather than freeze.

Visualization is neither mystical nor new; athletes have been using it in one form or another for years. A high jumper will pause prior to approaching the bar and mentally picture his approach, jump, and successful clearance. An Olympic weight lifter will pause before the barbell and momentarily visualize, in detail, the grasp, pull, split, and press.

Of course, along with the visualization, you must also practice physically. You can't visualize yourself into a perfect jumping back kick if you've never actually physically practiced it. But when you practice physically and mentally, your progress will be amazing.

As many top karate champions have discovered, visualization is a valuable asset to their training. It is an excellent device to add to your solo training to improve your self-image, achieve goals, and improve technique and tournament performance.

FEAR OF FAILURE

One of the major obstacles you face as a martial artist is the fear of failure. You will experience it from time to time, and it is important that you deal with it positively and not let it have a negative effect on your training and performance. Oftentimes the fear of failure will cause a stagnation or a regression in your progress; you want success, but you are afraid you will fail.

All fighters, even the so-called rated "top ten," can be affected by a fear of failure because they will undermine their training by putting too much importance on one single effort. If they do not win the tournament or pass the examination, they believe they have failed. The truth is that people who win trophies or progress in belt rank may not be exceptional, elite karate students. What they do have, though, is desire, discipline, determination, and the guts to risk failure—all necessary ingredients for personal success in the martial arts.

No one in karate has ever become successful without risk. Whether success is measured by achieving a stronger side kick or earning a higher belt, failure is an important part of the process of achieving that success. Understanding that failure is part of the process of growth is a big step toward eliminating fear.

Let us consider what failure isn't. Failure isn't judging yourself by the expectations of someone else. Your parents want you to win the match. "That's my boy," brags the father. "Kill him!" cheers the mother. Your instructor pressures you to win a trophy for the sake of the school. These often less-than-subtle expectations from other people put stress and a fear of failure in your mind that may negatively affect your performance. Even worse, you may decide not to compete at all out of fear of being subjected to someone else's disappointment or criticism.

Class peers and the general public are often quick to judge

you by the color of your belt. As a result, a belt examination is often a source of great fear. So rather than fail in the eyes of others, you choose not to take the test, or you may psych yourself with a fear of failure to such an extent that your performance will follow your negative mind-set. Failure should not be confused with living up to the expectations of others. Keep in mind that competing in the martial arts is self-discovery through the experience of facing yourself. Failure is not the act of losing a tournament or flunking a test. Failure is the act of not taking a risk at all.

If you want to enter the tournament and do so, or if you want to take the belt test and do—congratulations for trying; that is a success of a kind just because you took the risk. In time, facing that fear and taking the risk will produce results. At the very least, you will get more out of karate because risk-taking is growth.

When you stop to think about it, what is the worst that can happen if you fail? Your distorted sense of fear is probably far greater than its reality, since for the most part, failure is just a feeling of loss at the moment something occurs. Much the same is true of success. In reality, feelings of failure and success are just emotions that are part of the process of traveling the path of discovery.

It has been said many times that you learn more from your failures than you do from your successes, and it's true. I have many trophies in my basement that span years of competing. With some of them I just barely recall the tournament, let alone the win. I'm proud of them, of course, but sad that a few are just fading memories.

However, there are also empty places between trophies. They are empty becaue they represent tournaments where I didn't place high enough to win. I remember those tournaments quite well, because although I didn't win a gaudy piece of plastic, I did grow in my art. I grew because I learned something about karate, something about myself, and something about competing. My failures are rather like trophies, except they don't take up any room, gather dust, or fall over and break. Instead, they provide me with invaluable memories every time I look at the empty spaces.

Stay realistic about the whole concept of success and failure. Success doesn't guarantee great joy and happiness any more than failure should bring you great misery. Regardless of your wins and losses, keep in mind the benefits and pleasures you receive from the training. Also, be proud of how far you have come. Remember when you couldn't do a side kick without losing your balance?

Look at your failures as instigators to move you ahead. Every time you get knocked back a step, take two giant ones forward. Learn to keep moving and, in time, the word failure will take on an all-new meaning.

KEEPING MOTIVATED

No matter how motivated you are in the beginning, there will be times in your karate career when you will reach physical and mental plateaus, or worse, begin to regress. Usually the next stage is to skip a workout. When your mind gets to this point, it will continue to choose the easiest path, a path that usually stops at the television, sofa, fast food joint—anywhere but your training site. To stay enthused, you must pay close attention to how you are feeling physically and mentally. When you find yourself becoming disinterested and lackadaisical, it is time to evaluate why and decide what to do about it.

You may lack motivation because you are not progressing at the same rate you were in the first few months of your training. Let's say you have been training for about a year and have progressed through a couple of belt ranks. You can execute a variety of hand and foot techniques and can combine them into a relatively proficient sparring style. You are no longer overly concerned with the intricate mechanics of how to perform each movement.

Since you have adapted to the physical elements of the techniques, you may believe that if motivation is the key to successful karate, it must be easy to stay motivated once you no longer have to be concerned about the mechanics of the movements.

Now all you have to do is just keep on the same track and you will continue to improve at the same fast rate. Right? Wrong. The fact is, now that you can do the techniques fairly well, you will have to push longer and harder to see your improvements.

The quick rate of improvement at the beginning was enough motivation to keep you going. But once you have laid a good foundation, you will need to be creative physically and mentally in order to continue to progress.

If you are training hard every day, you can easily acquire burnout. Your body and mind need time to rest and recuperate. You cannot continue to push yourself day after day without your body becoming sluggish or even breaking down with injury or illness. When your mind becomes tired and stale, it begins to play the "skip a workout" game.

The opposite of overtraining is undertraining. If you have been going to class twice a week for a year and your progress is starting to slow or has even stopped, the cause may be from not training enough. This is because your body has adjusted to the physical demands of your workouts. You may be continuing to learn new techniques but your speed, power, and basics have not improved.

If you are losing motivation and becoming lax with your training, you can't help but be bored. Whether you are overtraining or undertraining, you need to get on the right track and get motivated again.

One of the best ways to get motivated is to take a week off from training to recharge yourself mentally and physically. Use this time to let your body rest and recuperate from any injury, and to tease yourself psychologically to create a hunger to resume training.

Usually by the third day your muscles will virtually itch to get back into training. This is a physical and mental sensation and is exactly what you want to happen. But don't give in to it and start training; let the desire build.

During the week, spend your free time reading karate books and magazines, watching full-contact karate on TV, going to Chinese kung-fu movies, and watching any training films or videos to which you have access. If you have photographs of yourself practicing or in competition, take them out and spend an evening placing them in a scrapbook.

The idea is to psych yourself with as much input as possible without yielding to the desire to train. You want to get yourself worked up to where you are bubbling with anticipation.

The next step is to look at your past training habits and see what modifications need to be made. If you have been overtraining, you need to limit yourself to a level within your capacity to progress. Bear in mind that if you are training to the extent where you are sore and tired every day, you are exceeding your capacity to recuperate and are risking injury and regression.

If you are going to your school every day, you need to cut back to three days, preferably every other day. Classroom workouts are most often of a general nature and consist of kata, sparring, self-defense drills, and basic technique. Three days of this is plenty. But if after a couple of weeks you find you are recuperating well and your energy is high, then you can add one day of solo training. Instead of adding another general school workout, you are adding a short training session in which you can specialize on any area you want. If after a while you feel you are physically capable of adding one more short solo workout, then do so. As a rule, however, you should never train more than five days a week because you need a minimum of two days to replenish yourself physically and mentally.

If you have been undertraining, you need to figure out a schedule so you can get one or two more workouts in during the week. If you can only train twice a week at your school, apply any of the solo training concepts taught in this book. Within a month you will be amazed at your progress because all that you needed was the specialization and extra training that a solo workout provides.

As is mentioned often in this book, martial arts is self-discovery. Learning to read yourself mentally and physically is one of the many benefits gained through karate study. By staying in tune to yourself, you will be able to detect when your motivation begins to weaken. When it happens, and it will, take a break, get yourself psyched, revamp your training schedule, and get going again.

Never, never, never, never, never, give up!

—Sir Winston Churchill

Chapter 2
Reps

Repetition training, or practicing reps as it is commonly called, is one of the easiest and most versatile ways to train by yourself. Rep practice can be done just about anywhere and can be applied to all areas of your karate training. Whether you are working on a singular technique, a combination of movements, or a kata, complete understanding will come only after thousands of reps.

ENTRENCHING THE TECHNIQUE
INTO THE SUBCONSCIOUS MIND

Remember the first time you were taught the reverse punch? You were taught how to make the stance, form the fist, and then all those complicated things about rotating your fist and retracting the opposite arm and not raising your shoulder and making sure you rotate your hip, and so on and so on. Your conscious mind was filled with a myriad of dos and don'ts, and you were embarrassed because your arms were waving about like a drunken symphony conductor.

But do you also remember how you looked two weeks later? Infinitely better. For two weeks you had been practicing that punch in class and at home. In your enthusiasm to learn, you probably fired off hundreds, perhaps thousands, of punches in those two weeks. As a result, those complicated steps began to move from your conscious mind into your subconscious.

When you first learned the punch, it seemed as if you had dozens of things to remember. Eventually, however, all of those repetitions helped you digest those steps into your subconscious, and within two weeks you could pop out a reverse punch without thinking. There may have been a couple of areas where you still had problems, but in time they smoothed out and joined the others in that mysterious section of your brain where actions are performed automatically.

The concept is similiar to typing. Imagine how long it would take to type one page if you had to consciously think how to sit, position your feet, and poise your hands over the keys; you look for the letter "k," peck, the letter "a," peck, and so on. Obviously this would never do. Good typing is done quickly, smoothly, and subconsciously. And so is punching.

Webster's defines *entrench* as "to establish securely." Whether you are just beginning karate or have years of experience, you need to practice reps to entrench the skills in your mind. Let's say you are working on a combination backfist, reverse punch, and front kick. If you are a beginner, you will need to consciously be aware of all the mechanics of the combination. As an advanced student, the technique may be easier to learn, but it will still involve conscious awareness of the mechanics.

No matter if you are advanced or a beginner, you must perform many reps to "establish securely" the combination in your subconscious mind. If you are advanced, you probably would entrench it more quickly than if you were a beginner, although this is not an absolute. Typically, an advanced student will eventually end up with a combination that is faster and stronger than a beginner's, just by virtue of the speed and strength he has developed in the past. However, merely being advanced does not guarantee you will entrench the technique faster than a beginner. Some people, no matter what their experience, simply take longer. The key is to train hard and perform lots of reps to achieve the end result, no matter what your experience.

The significance of getting the technique into the subconscious is that there is not enough time to think through all of the mechanics when sparring or defending yourself. The technique must be delivered quickly, smoothly, and with little or no thought. In fact, fighters are often surprised that they have no recall as to how they earned a tournament point or how they blackened an assailant's eye. This is a result of executing their techniques without conscious thought. Once this automatic action has been acquired and other factors, such as speed, timing, power, and explosiveness have been added, you will be well on your way to mastering the technique.

The value of practicing reps alone is that you can concentrate on the technique, break it down, analyze it, and single out any part that needs extra work. You are not controlled by an instructor or the needs of a class. You are in charge and you can conduct your training any way that you wish.

The following is one example of a solo, high-rep workout for the combination backfist, reverse punch, and front kick.

To entrench a combination into the subconscious, it must be broken down, analyzed, and repeated over and over. Try this movement. Execute a right backfist...

...followed by a reverse punch...

...and a left front kick. Then...

...retract the kick and assume your fighting stance.

Phase 1. The Combination without Footwork

Singular Techniques	Reps Each Side	Total Techniques Both Sides
Backfist	20	40
Reverse punch	20	40
Front kick	20	40
Total Singular Techniques:		120

Combining Two Techniques	Reps Each Side	Total Techniques Both Sides
Backfist, reverse punch	20	40
Reverse punch, front kick	20	40
Total Two Techniques:		80

Combining Three Techniques	Reps Each Side	Total Techniques Both Sides
Backfist, reverse punch, front kick	20	40
Total Reps Phase 1:		40

Phase 2. The Combination with Footwork

This phase involves using various methods of stepping while executing the combination. You can be as creative as you want in this phase because your objective is to practice the combination in as many foot patterns as possible. This will enhance your ability to execute the combination as well as broaden your understanding of the many applications of the technique. Some examples:

Performing The Combination With:	Reps Each Side	Total Techniques Both Sides
Lead leg lunge	15	30
Replacement step forward	15	30
Moving rear leg back	15	30
Replacement step backward	15	30
Combination Stepping:		
Lead leg lunge and backfist, replacement step forward, punch and front kick	15	30
Move rear leg back and backfist, replacement step backward, punch and kick	15	30
Total Reps Phase 2:		180

This simple program can be used for a singular hand or foot technique, or for even longer combinations than the example given here. Your goal is to entrench the technique into your subconscious using a method that is enjoyable and will prove beneficial when you are facing a live opponent.

DEVELOPING SMOOTH APPLICATION OF MOVEMENT

High-volume reps will help to smooth the execution of a technique. There is a world of difference between a white belt's and a black belt's roundhouse kick. Initially, the beginner's kick will be awkward, stiff, weak, and may even cause the kicker to lose balance. The black belt's roundhouse, however, will fire into the target as smoothly as a well-greased piece of machinery. With seemingly no effort, it will lift, arc, slam into the target, and then recoil with excellent form and grace.

The difference? Reps. By the time a martial artist has reached black-belt level, thousands of repetitions have been performed. In the process, all the muscles involved in the kick have become strengthened and flexible, allowing the muscles, ligaments, tendons, and joints to work together as a finely tuned instrument.

Advanced students should not cultivate the smug belief that high-rep training is only for beginners needing to smooth out techniques. Experienced students still need reps to maintain and progress. Once a particular skill level has been achieved through rep training, only continued training will maintain it. The muscles involved need the continual rep stimulus to maintain their strength, flexibility, and smoothness of movement. If rep training is discontinued, the adverse training effect occurs—loss of strength, speed, flexibility, and smoothness.

Through high-rep training, you are performing the specific movements that you want to develop. If you want to improve punching ability, you punch. If you want to increase your kicking skill, you kick. Jumping jacks is a fine exercise that stimulates the heart and tones the shoulders and legs, but it will do little to improve your kicking. If you want to develop general leg strength, you should do squats with some type of weight resistance. However, if you want a better side kick, you will develop it by performing side kicks.

DEVELOPING SPEED

No matter how strong you are, your strength will be useless if there is no speed behind it. If you have the power to bench-press 300 pounds but you are not fast enough to get a punch into the target, what good is your strength? You need both power and speed to be successful in your fighting ability.

There are different types of speed in karate. Reflex speed

is your ability to respond quickly to a stimulus such as an attack or an opening. Timing speed is your ability to time your attack in response to an opponent's action. A third type of speed is your ability to simply move your body quickly without any stimulus involvement. Developing the first two types of speed requires a training partner to coordinate action and reaction. However, the third type, raw limb speed, can be developed through solo training.

You can train by yourself with a concept of graduated speed reps to develop your basic speed. These are not mindless reps where you simply pop out rep after monotonous rep. To build your speed, you must concentrate and be cognizant of pushing each set faster than the last.

The graduated speed drill as taught in the Chuck Norris system is one of the best speed-development exercises you can do by yourself. Since the drill is graduated, it allows for total mental concentration and body awareness. Stages of the drill are arranged to take you through slow motion, half speed, full speed, and a final level called red-line.

Slow motion and half speed are levels that are first used to ensure that the technique is performed with optimum form, focus, rhythm, and balance. This is especially important if the technique is new or one that you have not practiced for a while. Also, it is a way of warming up physically and mentally to prepare for the faster movements.

The most common error is to leave the slow-motion and half-speed reps prematurely in order to get to the fast reps. Stay at these slower levels until you are absolutely ready to progress. What good is speed if you are not performing the technique properly?

Let's say you are practicing a backfist, turning back-kick combination. The slow-motion stage is a time to make sure all the fine points are in the technique. Your backfist is going out correctly and snapping at the end and retracting so that it aids your body's rotation into the turning back kick. The kick is straight and does not throw the body off balance, and your leg retracts properly and settles down to the floor in a solid fighting stance. These and other factors must be considered as you work out the "bugs" in slow motion.

Half speed is a step up from slow motion, so that you can see how the combination is coordinated at a greater speed. Be cognizant of the same factors you were in the slow-motion stage and correct any problems. Stay at half speed until the combination is performed smoothly and accurately.

Full-speed reps are performed as fast as you can do them without sacrificing proper form. It is important not to pop out the reps like a mindless piston but to concentrate on each technique and see the target clearly in your mind's eye. If you find that you are becoming sloppy, then slow down to half speed and recapture your form. As your form improves, go back again to full speed.

Red-line speed is where you go all out, forcing yourself to go faster and faster, pushing beyond what you think are your limitations. You may lose some of your form in red-line, but this is permissible in this phase for the sake of reaching toward greater speed.

There is no holding back in red-line. Force yourself; push yourself to make each rep faster than the last. This is as much a mental exertion as it is physical; reach inside your brain to force those reps at record speed. Work yourself into a controlled rage, use loud music, create a fantasy situation in your mind—use whatever it takes to fire out those red-line reps.

After your red-line set and after you have regained your breath, perform a final set at full speed. Since there is some form loss in the red-line set, a final set at full speed will allow you to finish the speed drill with good form.

Below is an example of a graduated speed drill:

Backfist, Turning Back Kick Combination	Reps Each Side	Total Reps Both Sides
Slow-speed	15	30
Half-speed	20	40
Full-speed	40	80
Red-line	15	30
Full-speed	10	20
Total Reps:		200

Raw limb speed can be developed by practicing the described graduated speed drill, but only if you push yourself beyond what you think are your limits. Try it with this combination. Fire out a left backfist...

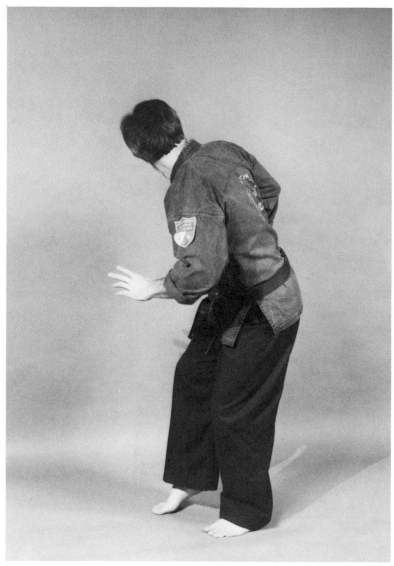

...then keep your eye on the target as you spin...

...into a back kick.

DEVELOPING POWER

Solo repetition training is an effective way to develop power in your basic technique. By performing the same technique that you want strengthened, you are working the specific muscles involved in that movement. This is not always true with weights and free-hand calisthenics, although both are valuable in a martial arts training program.

There are different types of power in karate. There is the power that comes from the velocity of the technique (the greater the speed, the greater the power). There is also a power that comes from a coordination of all the muscles with proper form at the right moment. This is called focus and requires much practice. This kind of power is derived from and limited by the strength in the muscles. In this section we will examine ways to develop power in the exact muscles involved in a given technique.

Developing the Kicking Muscles

An excellent method to develop kicking strength is to practice slow reps. Because in slow motion there is no body momentum, the muscles of the legs, hips, lower back, and abdominals are taxed to the maximum. In fact, you will know you are doing the reps correctly when your legs are quivering, your teeth are bared, and the cords in your neck are standing out boldly.

Front Kick and Side Kick, 2–3 Sets × 10 Reps Each

Raise the knee as high as possible, and then make a mental and physical effort to raise it even higher. Now, slowly proceed through the track of your kick, conscious of keeping your foot traveling as slowly and as high as possible. Hold your leg fully extended for a two-second count, and then slowly retract your foot on the same track and set it down. Perform the reps and sets with both legs.

A good way to develop power in the kicking muscles is to slowly perform the exact movement you want to strengthen. For the side kick, slowly lift your leg into the chambered position (upper left), and then physically, and mentally, lift it higher (upper right). Slowly push your kick out, hold for a moment (left), and then retract it.

Roundhouse Kick, 2–3 Sets × 10 Reps

Raise your leg into the chambered position so that your knee and foot are the same height. This maximizes the involvement of the hip muscles. Make a mental and physical effort to raise your chambered leg higher and higher. Slowly extend your leg through the track of your roundhouse kick, conscious of keeping your foot as high as possible. Hold your extended kick for a two-second count, and then slowly return it on the same track and set your foot down. Perform the reps and sets with both legs.

Back Kick, 2–3 Sets × 10 Reps

Raise your knee to the front, upper leg parallel to the floor. Slowly extend your leg through the track of your back kick, aiming with the heel of your foot. Hold your leg fully extended as you attempt to raise it even higher. Hold at your maximum height for a two-second count, and then slowly return your leg on the same track to your initial raised-knee position and set your foot down. Perform the reps and sets with both legs.

Key Points for Slow Kicking

1. Each rep should be performed s-l-o-w-l-y.
2. If a muscle painfully knots up, shake it out and proceed with the next step.
3. Minimize upper body bend when kicking. It may be easier to kick when you bend, but it cheats the muscles you want developed.
4. Practice slow kicking two or three times a week.

The Punching Muscles

You can work solo to increase the power of your hand techniques by tensing and relaxing the muscles. By repetitiously flexing the primary muscles involved in a particular hand strike, you will gain greater control of your body, increase the power of the technique, and improve your ability to focus your muscles upon impact with the target.

This is a tough exercise that is a little painful and energy-depleting, but it is also effective. Many students like to practice in front of a mirror without a shirt or while wearing a tank top in order to observe their muscles. If music helps psych you, turn on your favorite station and go to it.

To develop power in the punching muscles, begin with your left hand extended and your right hand chambered (left). Tense hard your fist and the muscles of your arms, back, chest, stomach, buttocks, and legs as you slowly extend your right fist and retract your left (right). Then...

...when you have completed the punch, tense your muscles as hard as you can and then relax.

Reverse Punch, 2–3 Sets × 8 Reps

Assume a left-leg-forward stance with your left arm extended slightly and your right fist at your hip. Slowly punch forward on the center line of your body, at shoulder height. As you punch, flex your fist, forearm, upper arm, latissimus dorsi (back muscle that flows into armpit), abdominals (stomach muscles), buttocks, and thigh muscles, and calf muscles.

Exhale as you punch and concentrate so that each of the muscles is working to its maximum. When your punch is extended, hold for a two-second count as you contract extra hard the four major areas: fist, latissimus dorsi, abdominals, and calves. Then immediately relax.

Backfist, 2–3 Sets × 8 Reps

Assume a left-leg-forward stance with your left arm cocked and your right fist at your solar plexus. Slowly execute a left-hand backfist while slightly inclining your body forward. As your fist is extended, contract your fist, forearm, upper arm, latissimus dorsi, upper chest abdominals, buttocks, thighs, and calves.

Once your arm is fully extended, tense extra hard the fist, latissimus dorsi, abdominals, and calves for two seconds. Relax, and retract your backfist to the starting position. Perform the reps and sets with both hands.

To develop the backfist muscles, tense all of the muscles of your arm as you slowly extend your fist. Then...

...when your arm is fully extended, tense extra hard the muscles on the back of the arm, especially around the elbow.

Key Points for Hand Techniques

1. Perform the reps slowly and contract the muscles hard.
2. Rotate your hips forward.
3. Lower your upper body into your abdominals as you rotate your hips.
4. Keep your shoulders down and your latissimus muscles flexed.
5. Do not hold your breath. Exhale on each rep.
6. Apply maximal contraction at the end of the movement to help develop focus.

Tensing through a movement will build strength and power in the exact muscles for that movement. The concept can be used with any hand technique, including blocks. It is not only effective for building power in techniques, but you will be delighted to find, as many students have, that you will develop a hard muscular physique as a result.

DEVELOPING EXPLOSIVENESS

An explosive technique is beautiful to watch, a thrill to deliver, and a real pain to the recipient. Many fighters confuse an explosive movement with one that has only great speed. This is only partly true. A technique that explodes has great speed combined with maximum power and perfect timing, and arrives without having been telegraphed.

Most often a technique will explode without conscious effort. This generally occurs when all of the above elements come together in a perfectly coordinated movement. Fighter A and fighter B square off, and A initiates a backfist. Like an exploding hand grenade, fighter B takes advantage of A's opening and slams a hard reverse punch into A's ribs. If the technique had been shot on ten frames of movie film, it would look as if the middle eight frames had been removed. All you would see would be a flicker of the fighting stances before B's scoring reverse punch.

A carefully watched sparring match will contain a lot of techniques, but only a few that are explosive. Under the pressures of point fighting, the tendency is to forget what you've been told and fight on instinct, using a few comfortable techniques. There are, however, repetition drills that will increase the frequency with which you explode under pressure.

A good drill you can work on by yourself is one taught by Dan Anderson in his American Freestyle system. He uses a method of lunging that is basically a "race" between hand and foot. This race generates an explosiveness that can easily be adapted to your punch, backfist, and ridge hand.

Assume a right-leg-forward fighting stance and lean your upper body forward so most of your weight is over your lead leg. Quickly scoot your lead foot forward a few inches and then immediately bring your rear leg forward so that you are back in your fighting stance. Practice this several times to get the correct feel.

To develop explosiveness, you must coordinate your hand and foot movements. A simple exercise to learn the footwork is to first assume a right-leg-forward fighting stance, with the majority of your weight on your lead leg (upper left). Then lean your upper body forward and quickly scoot your lead leg forward to maintain balance (upper right). Your rear leg immediately scoots forward, and you are back in your fighting stance (left).

The next stage is to coordinate the hand technique with the foot movement. Using a backfist, start your fist an instant before you move your forward foot. The technique flows in this order: fist starts; lead foot starts; fist hits; lead foot is still moving; fist snaps back; lead foot lands; and rear foot scoots forward. It is important to initiate your punch without any "telegraphing" (such as moving your shoulders or hips, shuffling your feet, or twitching your mouth). At one moment you're in a fighting stance; the next instant, you have thrown the punch.

Once you've developed the footwork, the next step is to coordinate the hand technique with your feet. Assume your fighting stance and start with your backfist...

...an instant before your lead foot moves. Then...

...when you are halfway through your lunge, your backfist hits the imaginary target...

...and is already retracting as your foot lands. Finally, ...

...your rear foot quickly scoots forward to assume your fighting stance.

The next step is to learn to cover a greater distance with your lead-leg lunge. Thrust your foot forward, driving with your rear leg and landing on the heel of your lead foot in order to get a solid foundation. Your rear foot scoots forward and lands solidly. The punch is executed just the same, moving the fist just before the foot, hitting the target, and snapping the punch back before the foot lands. The goal is to learn to move a considerable distance while maintaining good form and good body control.

The last stage is to throw two hand techniques before your foot lands. This could be a lead-hand jab followed by a reverse punch, or a backfist followed by a ridge hand, or a block followed by a counter. The combination is up to you. This is an advanced stage and should not be attempted until you feel confident with the other stages. Work hard to increase the speed of your forward leg thrust; in turn, that will force you to execute your hand techniques faster. Use a mirror to see that your hand techniques are going out and getting back before your foot lands.

Key Points for Developing Explosiveness

1. Do not telegraph your initial move.
2. Maintain a stone face and avoid looking directly at your target.
3. Keep your body relaxed prior to moving—especially the arms.
4. Think of the technique as a race between your hand and foot.

DEVELOPING ENDURANCE

You may have a devastating punch and a powerful side kick, but if you cannot endure the rigors of a lengthy sparring match or an all-out street fight, your techniques may be ineffective. By strengthening your heart and lungs through the practice of high-volume reps, you will have greater stamina and, as a result, improve your performance and your progress.

Improved endurance is derived from developing a strong cardiovascular system—the heart, lungs, and blood vessels. Chapter Five will explain, in detail, various methods of modifying your style to fit the specific requirements of a cardiovascular exercise.

Some fighters like to jog, while others complain that the cardiovascular effect from roadwork does not overlap to the dojo or the tournament ring. Repetition training, however, can easily be made to fit the requirements of a cardiovascular exercise. Reps can be performed using any of the methods already mentioned in this chapter, or you can try the sample workout below. What is important is that your heart rate be elevated and maintained at a high level for at least fifteen minutes.

Endurance Workout Using Reps	Time (min.)
Front kick, right kick	1
Front kick, left kick	1
Roundhouse, right leg	1
Roundhouse, left leg	1
Side kick, right leg	1
Side kick, left leg	1
Back kick, right leg	1
Back kick, left leg	1
Replacement step, right reverse punch	1
Replacement step, left reverse punch	1
Left backfist, right reverse punch	1
Right backfist, left reverse punch	1
Left roundhouse kick, right turning back kick	1
Right roundhouse kick, left turning back kick	2
Left lead head block, right reverse punch, right front kick	2
Right lead head block, left reverse punch, left front kick	2
Total Time:	19

The intensity and number of the repetitions depends on how hard you want to work. If you want to work at 60 percent of your maximum heart rate, you will be performing fewer reps at an easier pace. Working at 80 percent means you will perform the reps harder and more often. (A formula for determining your optimum aerobic heart rate appears in the chapter on cardiovascular training.)

Working to improve your endurance by practicing reps gives you the advantage of conditioning your heart and lungs specifically for the special demands of karate or kung fu. In addition, you can work on your speed, strength, form, footwork, recovery, and coordination while improving your endurance.

DEVELOPING DISCIPLINE/GOAL SETTING

The martial arts require discipline. Daily training when tired, injured, or ill requires a tremendous amount of willpower. The student who pushes on, refusing to allow obstacles to get in the way, will find himself reaching new heights in skill and arriving at a new concept of self.

Rep training is an excellent tool to help you along this path. Reps are not only effective for improving technique, but also as tools to push yourself physically and mentally beyond your preconceived capabilities. One of the purposes of this book is to try to make solo training interesting and productive. But there will be times when training by yourself will be difficult. Those are the times when you must dig deep within yourself to find whatever it takes to push on. Reps can be a very important ladder to personal martial arts growth.

Let us say you have set a short-term daily goal of performing the four basic kicks, front, round, back and side, 100 times each kick with each leg. How you set up the reps is entirely up to you: combinations, sets of ten, sets of 50, kicks alternated with punches, or whatever. What is important is that you perform all the kicks, a total of 400 with each leg, before you allow yourself to complete your workout.

The next step is to discipline yourself to reach the goal and push on. You must push on no matter how it hurts. Your brain is the boss, not the pain; you are the master of the goal; you must succeed. Even if one day you set your goal unrealistically high, *do not change it* halfway through. Your body will invariably seek the easy route. Your legs will want to kick slowly, and they may even try to convince you to sprawl on the sofa. Do not listen. You cannot be denied your goal. You must discipline your brain to win out over your body so that each rep is as high, sharp, and fast as the one before.

If you weaken and give up on your short-term goal because you are tired, bored, or just lazy, then you should feel uncomfortable and guilty about your decision. You are responsible for your success or failure, and if you quit, you have let yourself down. Only yourself.

Many fighters complain because they believe they do not have the discipline to train by themselves. Setting a short-term reachable goal of so many repetitions in just one solo workout is a good way to begin building the necessary self-discipline. When you become comfortable with short efforts, you can progress to a week-long goal using repetitions as your tool.

Say, for example, you may want to work on a particular kata in preparation for an upcoming tournament. You have set a tough goal, but not an impossible one, of performing the form 100 times during the next week.

Below is an example of kata performed in high reps during one week:

Days	Reps
Mon.	5
Tues.	20
Wed.	5
Thurs.	25
Fri.	5
Sat.	25
Sun.	15
Total:	100

Since you attend class on Monday, Wednesday, and Friday, you have wisely decided you will practice the form only five times after class because of the fatigue factor from your other training. Your "classless" days are solo-training days when you will work only on the kata. If one day you have to cut your workout short because of other obligations, you must then make up for it the next day. Your goal is 100 reps for the week, and you are disciplining yourself to win your battle no matter how you have to juggle the days around.

You can practice the reps in a variety of ways. The kata can be performed at slow, medium-fast, or fast speeds. You can break it into sections and perform each grouping of movements five to ten times before moving onto the next section. It doesn't matter how you do it, so long as you benefit from the exercise and progress toward your goal of 100 repetitions.

When you go through that 100th and last time, you will feel great because you and only you have won the battle. You now know that you have the discipline and the courage not to quit. You have developed the discipline and the fortitude to fight the battle no matter how tough it may be.

Interestingly, the discipline developed from high-rep drills will not only help in your overall martial arts studies, but will overlap to other areas of your life. You will find that this new-found discipline, this new awareness of yourself, will help you at school, on the job, and in personal relationships. Formerly insurmountable problems will shrink to mere pebbles in your path.

Chapter 3

Environmental Training

It is easy to get in a rut of always training in the same place day after day. There are black belts who have trained for years but have never ventured outside their school doors. They are good at what they do, but do they have a complete understanding of how well, or how poorly, their art functions in other environments?

It is one thing to perform a spinning hook kick in a wide-open, well-lit training hall and quite another to throw the kick at night, on wet pavement, standing between two parked cars, and while wearing tight jeans. If you have only practiced in your school, how do you know your art will work elsewhere under different circumstances?

Training in different environments will not only expand your knowledge, experience, and creativity, but it will greatly increase your enjoyment of practicing your martial art. Out of the confines of your school, you can experiment with your techniques in various settings that are completely remote from your normal training. Through experimentation, you will increase your understanding of your art's limitations and strengths; by challenging yourself in a variety of environments, you will discover much about your own strengths and weaknesses.

TRAINING IN THE DARK

Training in total darkness will increase your understanding of balance and proper form. When there is no light, you are deprived of visual perspective in relation to your surroundings, and therefore must rely on how your body feels as it moves. If you do not have this feel, you will have little control of your movements, your punches will be off center, your stances will be askew, and your kicks all but useless.

Total darkness will create an intense awareness of yourself because there is nothing visual to distract or assist with what you are doing. You are practicing in a black void where space is reduced to what you can sense and direction is difficult to determine. Therefore, it will be necessary for you to concentrate on each movement and clearly visualize what you are doing as you are doing it. As you perform your movements, you must learn to see the techniques like a movie projector shining in the darkness, relying on the feel of your body to duplicate what you see.

There are two ways to visualize the technique. You can quickly see the move in your mind an instant before you do it, which provides a moving picture as a guide just prior to your actual performance of the technique. The second method is to visualize the technique as you simultaneously perform it physically. Try both methods separately to see which you prefer; you may even want to combine both methods.

Practicing kata in the dark can be as difficult as it is fun. If your form has fast changes in direction, high kicks, and jump kicks, you will undoubtedly experience balance problems. Use visualization techniques to clarify your movements and to help you maintain your equilibrium.

Shadowboxing an imaginary opponent is a good exercise and one that is a lot of fun in the dark. Move about while throwing punches, kicks, and blocks—all the while being cognizant of good execution, recovery, footwork, stances, and most of all, balance. Keep the images racing through your mind and concentrate hard on precise form in the performance of your technique.

Training in the dark epitomizes solo training. Since you are in total darkness, your entire environment is reduced to just yourself, and you must rely on body feel and images projected in your mind. Although you will feel strange and awkward at first, in time your mind and body will work as a unit. The result will be that you will move a little further ahead toward a complete understanding of balance, body movement, and how the mind and body work together.

TRAINING WITH MUSIC

Training alone to music is fun, productive, and surprisingly painless. More than just having a radio on somewhere in the background, you will need music that has a loud, upbeat sound that you can feel and move to as you synchronize your techniques.

Shadowboxing is a good exercise that is quite adaptable to music. It is an exercise of sparring by yourself as you move about throwing punches, kicks, and blocks in order to develop footwork and body movement, improve basic technique, and strengthen the cardiovascular system.

Select music that has a definite, pronounced beat, and turn up the volume until you are engulfed by the sound. Begin to move about as if you were sparring and let the music carry you in and out of range of your imaginary opponent. Time the execution of your blocks, kicks, and punches so that you are responding to the pronounced beat of the music.

Initially, you may feel a little silly shadowboxing to music. Eventually, however, you will find yourself moving rhythmically to the sounds, and delivering attacks and blocks with an improved flow and coordination. Even though shadow boxing is a solo exercise, the benefits you'll gain will carry over to your regular sparring.

Shadowboxing to music is an enjoyable way to improve your endurance by systematically strengthening your cardiovascular system. Choose a record that is long enough to give you at least fifteen minutes of solo sparring, and maintain this elevated heart rate (see Chapter Five for criteria) throughout the session.

Practicing your kata to music will enhance your enjoyment of your form and help you establish a rhythm and mood. It is important to select music that isn't just in the background, but on the contrary, significantly affects how you perform the kata physically and mentally. The mood you choose can be one that is light and fun, full of energy and excitement, or heavy with the drama of battle.

When you are choosing music, listen carefully with your kata in mind and ask yourself if the beat fits in with your punches and kicks. Do the musical pauses coincide with the dramatic pauses in your kata? Does the music slow where your movements slow; does it suddenly explode when you explode with a flurry of techniques? The music needs to be carefully chosen so that it complements your form and is precisely related to your movements. Choose wisely and you will experience an improved kata, an enjoyment of physical movement and an exciting solo workout.

Interestingly, karate training to music is virtually painless—at least until the workout is over. The effect is similar to that of dancing in that the music blocks the fatigue. If you were at a dance where there was no music but you still danced around as if there were, you would tire very quickly. However, if music were added (not to mention an attractive partner), you could dance all night. Practicing your martial art to music is no different because the music will lift your spirit and increase your training enjoyment, as well as improve your endurance, reflexes, rhythm, and overall martial skills.

TRAINING WHILE WATCHING TV

Training while watching TV? The very thought of it is blasphemy to the staunch traditionalists who feel that training must be conducted only in the most sterile of environments. They will advocate training in the dojo, a forest, or

Time spent watching TV can also be time spent stretching.

under a waterfall—but while watching TV? Never!

We watch a lot of television in this country. Statistics indicate each of us watches the tube an average of four hours per day. These are hours spent lying on the sofa, mindlessly staring at programs we won't remember the next day.

For the most part, TV-watching is dead time. Usually you move twice, once to go to the bathroom and once to load up on snacks. In the process, your muscles have become sluggish, your brain has turned to mush, and your stomach has taken in 2,000 calories of pop, chips, and other assorted non-foods. The time has been wasted and nothing has been gained.

Since few television shows require 100 percent of your attention, why not use the viewing time to do something toward advancing your skill in the martial arts? You can work on stretching, calisthenics, or any techniques that are easy to do while dividing your attention with the tube.

Your stretching routine is one of the easiest and most productive exercises you can do in front of the set. The atmosphere is more relaxed than the dojo and you are not forced to hurry through the stretches, as is often the case in class. You can take your time, hold the stretches as you like, and even try some new ones. If you are tired from a long day at work or school, the stretching will increase your circulation and release energy into your system. You will feel awake and energized, plus you will have worked on your much-needed flexibility exercises—all while watching TV.

Push-ups, sit-ups, weightless squats, and holding static stances are simple exercises that are easy to do in front of the television. You can do quite a few push-ups during a rerun of *I Love Lucy*, and as a result develop stronger arm and chest muscles. A goal of 50 sit-ups during every two-minute commercial will add up to 200 at the end of a thirty-minute program. Instead of developing flab from all those dashes to the refrigerator, you will develop a hard, tight midsection.

Holding deep static stances will make your stances stronger and more stable and help develop your legs for kicking. An interesting exercise is to sit in a horse stance or assume a forward stance every time there is a two-minute commercial. Your long-term goal can be to develop enough leg strength to hold a stance during the program and then rest during the commercial. Imagine how strong your legs would be today if you had started this six months ago.

Although you can practice techniques in front of the tube, you should not choose movements that require your total attention, such as new techniques or complicated ones. Keep your techniques simple and fun. For example, instead of sitting in your easy chair, try kicking over the back of it 50 times with each leg, or move around in your fighting stance and pop 100 backfists at the screen. See how many side kicks you can throw during each commercial, or push the furniture back and practice small sections of your kata.

Practicing while watching TV is not something to do to make solo training easier for yourself. It is permissible, however, when you just can't bring yourself to train any other way, or whenever you get the urge to practice a little right in the middle of your favorite show. Compared with not training at all, training while watching TV is a desirable option.

TRAINING IN CRAMPED QUARTERS

You probably train in a school where there is ample space to spar, practice kata, and work on various drills. However, street self-defense situations typically occur in a parking lot between two cars, in a crowded bar surrounded by tables and chairs or squeezed among gyrating dancers. Since you are more likely to be assaulted in a phone booth or a service-station restroom than in an open field, you should spend some time training in these kinds of environments. Not only is doing so a relevant workout, but it is also an interesting variation of your solo-training experience.

Choose a room in your home or dojo that is cluttered with furniture, boxes, or stacks of newspapers, or any place that is limited in space. Do not move things around or in any way make the space comfortable, because the more miserable the space, the better it is for this type of training.

In your new "dojo," you can practice anything you want: reps, combinations, footwork—just about anything except possibly your kata, at least not in its entirety. This is a time to be creative, to analyze how you would fight in a small cluttered space.

How would you adjust your techniques in the following situations? Your back is to the wall and you can't position your fist at your hip because your elbow will hit the wall. You are pressed against a pantry shelf and you cannot lean your upper body back to kick. An imaginary assailant swings a board at you from the other side of a stack of pop bottles.

In many situations it will be impossible to use your favorite techniques. Instead of a roundhouse kick, you will have to use a knee strike; instead of a blow with your ridge hand, you may find that you can use the clutter to your advantage. Perhaps you can hang from a ceiling pipe and kick; you can grab a box and use it as a shield and then employ it as a weapon to counterattack.

Although there will be many environmental problems with which you will have to contend, the longer you experiment and practice, the more and better the options you will create. Training in a small, crowded environment is fun and revealing. You will learn what can and cannot be done.

TRAINING ON STAIRS

Solo training on stairs is as enlightening as training in a small space. It is a definite change of pace from your regular training and will force you to think more than usual about body movement. You will especially have to pay attention to footwork and stance limitations that may affect your techniques.

There are several physical characteristics of stairs that should be considered.

Width of the Steps

The width of each individual step is important because it affects the stability of your stances. If the steps are seven inches wide and you wear a size-ten shoe, you will find a decided lack of stability in most positions. You will need to examine how to move forward, backward, sideways, and up and down while executing kicks, punches, and blocks.

You will need to analyze body movement and footwork when trying your techniques on various types of stairs.

The Number of Steps

Training where there are only three steps provides a different experience than training halfway up a twenty-step stairwell. With three steps, you can leap to the top one for a quick height advantage or you can jump to the floor to make your escape. However, with a larger stairwell, you must contend with many steps below and above you.

Handrails

If the stairwell has handrails, you can experiment to determine if they can be used to your advantage. Try throwing side kicks at an imaginary opponent above you while holding onto the railing for support. If there are rails on both sides of the stairs, grasp both of them and thrust various kicks downward at an opponent on a lower step.

Narrow Stairwell

A stairwell that is so narrow that your shoulders barely clear the walls will present different options from one that is very wide. If your attacker is on roughly the same level, you might experiment with elbows and knees. If the attacker is below or above you, you will find straight kicks more effective than circular ones.

Use your imagination and creativity when training on stairs. Analyze the setting and determine how best you can fight given the circumstances. When you have worked out the solution, practice the techniques often. Place yourself in a variety of situations and stay with each one until you can respond to each with speed, power, and balance.

Training on stairs will not only provide you with variety in your solo training but will prepare you mentally in the event you are faced with a real self-defense situation in a similar environment.

Environmental Training

TRAINING OUTDOORS

Ideally, solo outdoor training is practiced deep in the wilderness, but students living in a large city may not have access to the wild. A similar environment, however, may be found in a large city park, a cluster of trees, a large garden, or even a rooftop nursery. Although there are a few characteristics that are required, the experience is largely a mental one.

Solo training outdoors is a fun and beneficial way to train that just might become habit-forming. Alone, in the soft, quiet world of nature, you will be invigorated mentally as well as physically. The sounds, sights, and feelings of the natural environment will lift you spiritually, energize you physically, and move you into closer contact with your art, yourself, and nature.

Take the time to enjoy your surroundings before you begin training. Feel the sun, breathe in the fresh air, and smell the clean, green scent of the grass and trees. Listen to the silence as you breathe in slowly and deeply, letting your tensions ebb, and your whole body relax and ready itself for training.

Once you are relaxed, begin by stretching your muscles, using your regular routine and deliberately taking your time for each stretch. Use this time not to push for a maximum range, but to simply enjoy a comfortable stretch to release energy and invigorate your entire body. Concentrate on your muscles and bask in the warm sun or the cool shade, letting your body slowly respond to the heat or coolness.

After your muscles are stretched and tingling with anticipation for the training, begin with slow kata practice. This provides you with an enjoyable transition from stretching into your martial art, while still uniting your body with nature. The slow movements allow you to concentrate on your form and to continue to draw inspiration from the beauty of your surroundings.

Practicing the form slowly and deliberately does not mean

that it lacks intention or is done halfheartedly. Indeed, this is a time to put maximum fighting spirit into the blocks, kicks, and punches. Because the kata is performed slowly, it is more a mental exercise that a physical one.

Breathe in deeply, as if you were drawing in strength from the wind, the sun, and all of nature. Proceed slowly with the first movement and feel the power flow from your attack or block into the imaginary target. Move slowly from stance to stance, concentrating deeply and moving precisely as you execute technique after technique.

Visualize your power as wind roaring out of your fists and feet, wind you have gathered from nature and converted into an awesome and destructive force that you are driving into your opponents. Tense your muscles at the end of each movement to focus all that force, for one brief instant, into the target. Relax, breathe in, and flow to the next technique. Continue until you have finished the form, and then pause for a moment as you continue breathing deliberately to recharge your body with nature's energy.

Performing slow kata outdoors is a kind of moving meditation. You are concentrating on each movement, visualizing each and every technique as you simultaneously perform the movements physically. The involvement of the mind with your body will create a sense of softness, sensitivity, and awareness which will result in a very pleasant, flowing state of meditation.

Besides the mental and spiritual benefits of training outdoors, the variety of terrain will provide a diverse and interesting training ground for practicing basic technique. The tendency is to find a place that is spacious, with a clean and unobstructed surface on which to train. This is fine, sometimes. To add more realism and to more fully understand your art, especially the footwork, try practicing on the following types of terrain: rocks; the side of a hill; sand; shallow water; a cluster of trees; tall grass; on or around fallen trees; and rough and uneven ground.

Thoroughly examine the terrain and determine what

Practicing kata outdoors is fun, invigorating, and educational.

Examine the effectiveness of your stances on a variety of surfaces. Can your stationary foot pivot on rough and uneven terrain?

Examine your balance and stability when executing a simple hand technique such as a backfist and reverse punch combination.

techniques are practical. Many factors need considering. What hand techniques can you use or not use? Can you rotate your support foot while kicking? How effectively can you move from stance to stance? Do you have to modify your hand techniques to compensate for slower foot movements? Should you ever have to defend yourself outdoors, these are the sorts of problems you will have to solve.

Your practice can consist of repetition training using a variety of singular and combination techniques. Shadowboxing is another fun and revealing exercise that will give you some ideas of how a battle would go. As you move about the terrain attacking and defending against imaginary opponents, be sure to pick a location where you are alone. You may look a little strange to the public, swinging from tree limbs and rolling down grassy slopes.

Each type of terrain will necessitate that you modify and adapt your normal style of throwing punches and kicks. The more you examine and experiment, the greater your understanding of your art as well as the entire concept of fighting in other that an ideal environment.

TRAINING IN THE RAIN

Training in the rain is a wonderful variation on outdoor training that is both spiritually uplifting and physically beneficial. A cool mist or a thundering downpour will add a new and enjoyable dimension to your solo training.

As with all outdoor training, you will learn new things about your old techniques. It's one thing to practice on a dry dojo floor and quite another on wet grass. You will discover that your footwork will need to be adjusted to compensate for the wet surface. Those flashy high kicks will be more risky when your support foot is on grass, wood, rocks, or cement that is wet and slippery.

How you train in the rain is up to your imagination and needs. You can work on basic kicks, punches, kata, attack and defense combinations, and shadowboxing. You might want to consider training nonstop for a good endurance session so that you can get your workout over and get out of the rain to prevent getting chilled.

You should warm up thoroughly before you go out into the rain. Once you are outside, get right to your workout because it is important to stay warm and keep your muscles loose. When you have completed your training, immediately go back inside and change into dry clothing. Finish your workout by doing a few stretches for the legs, back, and arms so that your body gets a proper cool-down. Afterward, have a shower; put on some warm, dry clothes, and have a hot beverage. You'll feel like a million.

Psychologically and spiritually, practicing in the rain at a nearby park, backyard, or, especially, in the wilderness will be an experience impossible to achieve anywhere else. You will experience a feeling of being part of the outdoors: the sounds of the splattering rain, rustling leaves, and whispering winds. With only the sounds of your breathing, your movements, and the sounds of the storm, you will experience a blending of nature, self, and martial art.

TRAINING IN WATER

Training in water is fun and will give you a hard workout for the specific muscles involved in kicking and punching. It doesn't matter if it's done in a swimming pool, river, lake, or ocean, as long as the water is deep enough to cover your shoulders and provide resistance against your movements.

Performing 15 roundhouse kicks underwater, for example, will place a tremendous amount of resistance on the kicking leg throughout the range of motion. You will experience various muscles of the leg, hip, and lower back coming into play that you never thought were involved in the kicking process. In addition, the muscles of the supporting leg will be affected as they work harder to maintain balance.

It is surprising how many muscles are stimulated when you perform a simple movement such as a backfist. After you have performed a few sets, you will feel a definite burning sensation in the shoulders, specifically the lateral side, and the triceps muscles, located on the back of the arm. This so-called "burning" is a sensation that professional bodybuilders seek in order to stimulate maximum muscle growth.

Moving in the water provides resistance throughout the entire range of the technique so that strength and speed are developed both in the direction of the attack and the retraction. This is not always the case with conventional bodybuilding equipment or free-hand exercises. In a push-up, for example, you can cheat on your descent. Underwater exercises provide continual resistance.

The following routine will exercise the primary muscles involved in the performance of various techniques:

Technique	Direction of Force	Primary Muscles	Sets + Reps
Backfist	Diagonal	Shoulders, triceps	3 × 10
Forward punch	Forward	Shoulders, chest, back	3 × 10
Roundhouse punch	Circular	Shoulders, waist	3 × 10
Hammer fist	Downward	Back, shoulders	3 × 10
Upper cut	Upward	Shoulders, biceps	3 × 10
Front kick	Forward	Thighs	3 × 8
Side kick	Sideward	Hips, lower back, buttocks	3 × 8
Roundhouse kick	Circular	Hips, lower back, thighs	3 × 8
Back kick	Backward	Lower back, buttocks	3 × 8
Hook kick	Circular	Hips, back of thighs	3 × 8

Practiced consistently, this routine will give you a substantial workout and increase your power, speed, and balance. During the first week, do only one set and increase one set each week until you have reached three. Next, increase the intensity by increasing the speed of the techniques or by reducing the rest period between each set and exercise.

Practicing your kata underwater is a unique way to strengthen each individual technique as well as develop strong, solid stances. Although you can practice the kata in its entirety, a better way is to break the form down into sequences and perform only a few movements at a time. When you go through one sequence five times in a row, you are better able to concentrate on just a few movements and those specific muscles involved. When you have finished one sequence, move on, in chronological order, to the next sequence, and so on to the end of the form. If you practice this two or three times a week, you will discover a big difference in your speed and power.

Working out in the water is an especially enjoyable way to train solo in the summer, when the very thought of working out by yourself in the stifling heat is often enough to make you sit in the shade and drink a cold soda.

Chapter 4
Kata

Practicing kata alone provides you with a time for physical refinement of the movements and for enhancing your understanding of each technique and its relationship to the entire form. It is also a time when you can let your creative juices flow and apply your own personal style and interpretation.

It is important that you completely understand your kata technically before you apply any of the concepts mentioned in this chapter. It makes no sense to drill hard on various physical and mental skills if your basic techniques are incorrect. First learn the form correctly and then proceed with the following suggestion.

Begin thinking of your kata as a play. It has all the elements: a beginning, final scene, and several scenes in between. It has a protagonist—you the defender—and it has antagonists— the multiple attackers; you are the hero, they are the villains. As with any play, your kata should contain emotion, mood, spirit, and a feeling of creativity. In short, kata is theater.

As in all quality theater, your play must be believable. And credibility begins in your mind. You must perform as if you were in a real battle with multiple attackers—feel them, see them, understand what they are doing, and fight back with the knowledge of how your blocks and counters apply to your advantage in the scene.

Many martial artists race through their forms as if in a hurry to get on to something else. They toss their techniques out with no apparent grasp of what they represent. Their kicks and punches are simply flipped out with little or no power, speed, or focus—as if they were cheerleaders performing a complicated but silly pep routine, instead of warriors training for a life-and-death battle.

Fill your play with emotion and spirit. Many kata performers show more emotion eating a sandwich than they do with their form. Showing emotion doesn't mean mugging like an old-time comedian; however, some facial exressions are involved. For realism, watch the facial expressions of your fellow students as they spar and be aware of your own as you work out with a partner. Your face will show a reaction to your opponent's sudden kick and will show intensity as you fire back a counterpunch.

Although as a martial artist you have control over your emotions, you will still express them to some degree with your face. Your expressions will supplement the intensity of your techniques, especially if the expressions are real. Since reality comes from your mind, if you truly believe the fight, your facial expressions will naturally reflect your emotion. When your mind believes there is a fight and your face reflects that belief, your techniques will increase in intensity.

Let your fighting spirit come out in your mock battle. You are not washing your socks, but engaged in a survival situation. Feel the warrior within you. Feel it in your stances, breathing, shout, eyes, and techniques. Believe that you are a samurai, a Ninja, a warrior fighting for your life while maiming and killing others. Find your spirit, and bring it to your battle.

Like a play, your kata contains numerous scenes. A scene is your involvement with one specific confrontation. Most of the time this involves one attacker, although it could be two or three, depending upon the kata. Most forms begin

Let the intensity of your kata reflect in your eyes.

Believe in the battle and your body will show strength and the emotion of the fight.

with a block or defensive movement followed by a counter-attack; that is your first scene. You then turn to block or attack a new opponent coming from a different direction; that is scene two. For scene three, turn 180 degrees and attack, block, block, and counterattack two opponents. This continues until you have successfully gone through all the scenes of your play and are standing victorious but exhausted at the end.

Many kata performers fail to see the scenes and just rush through their forms as if they were one long multiple technique, not understanding where one opponent ends and the other begins. It adds realism and drama to your kata when, after concluding with one attacker, you pause to see, or sense, the next attacker. As with music, the pauses are just as significant as the movements. You can experiment by performing two or more scenes together without a pause, and then performing them with a pause to determine which feels and looks the best.

You may interpret the form as follows: blend scenes one and two, then pause briefly; blend scenes three and four, then pause briefly; perform only scene five with a long pause; blend scenes six, seven, and eight, then pause briefly; and so on through the entire form. You may interpret the form a little differently each time you practice, or you may always do it exactly the same way. It doesn't really matter, nor does it dramatically change the form—even a traditional one. The techniques stay the same, but your creativity changes the interpretation.

An effective approach to improving your kata is to isolate each individual scene. If you have blended scenes together, they will count as only one scene for this particular exercise. Begin with your first scene and practice it five to ten times, then proceed to the next scene for the same number of reps. Continue through the form, scene after scene, until you have completed all of them.

This method of training has several advantages. It narrows your concentration to one small segment of the form and enables you to put more intensity into the movements. You are able to put greater strength and speed into the small cluster of techniques and concentrate more on the drama and emotion you want in each scene.

If you are having a problem with a technique, you will be more able to clarify and correct it when you are performing a single scene. The faulty technique is easily isolated, analyzed, and corrected by having concentrated on only one small segment of the form.

Practicing your kata in scenes is one of the fastest methods of improving your overall performance. Many kata competitors will train using the scene concept and not perform their kata in their entirety until the day before the tournament. Others will practice each scene several times and then go through the entire form a few times during each workout. It doesn't matter how you do it as long as your method works for you.

One of the biggest problems about repetition training is trying to maintain concentration. This is even more of a problem when you are practicing a lengthy kata, especially if you have been practicing it for a long time. The better you know it, the more difficult it is to stay mentally focused. Scene training helps in that it is much easier to stay mentally and physically committed to a scene ten times than it is to perform an entire kata ten times.

Practicing kata alone is a time to use your imagination and creativity so as to give it life and increase your enjoyment. Approaching it as a play in which a real battle is occurring is one method. Other concepts mentioned in this book, such as training outdoors, in the dark, and to music will help your mental and physical commitment.

Chapter 5

Cardiovascular Training

Physical fitness is not only one of the most impor-
tant keys to a healthy body, it is the basis of dynamic
and creative activity. The relationship between the
soundness of the body and the activities of mind
is subtle and complex. Much is not yet understood.
But we do know what the Greeks knew: that intel-
ligence and skill can only function at the peak of
their capacity when the body is healthy and strong;
that hearty spirits and tough minds usually inhabit
sound bodies.

—John F. Kennedy

It is commendable that you have a powerful punch. It is
also good that you can pump out forty push-ups. These
abilities, however, are not true indicators of your physical
fitness. Muscular fitness is important to you, but it is too
limited a measure of your martial arts abilities and overall
fitness in that it pertains to only one system of the body, and
therefore has a limited beneficial effect on the important
organs and overall health. Endurance fitness should be your
goal not only as a karate student but as a person seeking
good health and fitness. In fact, it is the foundation on which
you should base your fitness level.

A cardiovascular exercise is any activity that stimulates the heart and lungs for a period of time. It is necessary that the exercise elevates the heart rate and causes the lungs and arteries to work at a level that is not their maximum capacity, but one that is carried out for a prolonged period.

Through cardiovascular exercise you are working to improve how your body uses oxygen. In order for you to punch, kick, and spar, you first need energy, and to supply that energy, you need food. Oxygen burns, or metabolizes, the food you eat in order to provide calories for energy. Unlike food, however, your body cannot store oxygen and must continually replenish its supply.

When you have developed a higher level of cardiovascular fitness, your lungs will be conditioned to process more air with less effort. Therefore, when you are having an exhausting workout, say, a heavy sparring session, you will use nearly twice as much air every minute than a person not in good cardiovascular condition. Your conditioned body is being provided with more oxygen, which in turn will produce more energy for harder training.

You will develop a strong and healthy heart once your cardiovascular system has developed a greater level of fitness. Your heart will be extremely efficient, pumping with less exertion a greater quantity of blood with each heartbeat. Consequently, because it pumps a higher volume of blood with each stroke, it will beat less often. The conditioned athlete who exercises consistently has a resting heart rate of around 60 beats or fewer per minute. Typically, those who do not train have a resting heart rate of 80 or more beats per minute. Look at the following comparison.

Sixty beats per minute, times sixty minutes, equals 3,600 beats per hour. Multiplying this by twenty-four hours equals 86,400 beats per day. By contrast, 80 beats per minute, times sixty minutes, equals 4,800 beats per hour. Multiplying this by twenty-four hours equals 115,200 beats per day.

Even at complete rest, the heart of a person who is not in condition will beat nearly 30,000 times more every day.

Add some fairly strenuous activity, such as throwing a few easy punches or kicks, and the out-of-shape heart will experience a higher rate of increased heartbeats than the conditioned heart experiencing the same activity. Even during sleep the conditioned heart will beat 20 times less per minute than the out-of-condition one. This adds up to a savings of 10,000 beats during one night's sleep.

Another major benefit of cardiovascular fitness for the karateka is improved blood flow, or tissue vascularization. Improved vascularization is an essential factor in increasing endurance and reducing fatigue in the muscles by saturating the tissues with energy-producing oxygen.

Since vascularity begins in the heart, the heart may actually increase in size as it becomes more cardiovascularly fit. Interestingly, there are two kinds of enlarged hearts. One is the so-called "athlete's heart," and the other is one that has become enlarged because it is out of condition and needs to compensate for some deficiency in the cardiovascular system or elsewhere. Its interior volume, despite its exterior size, is small, and as a result cannot pump much blood.

The athlete's heart, however, is strong and healthy, is relatively large, and works efficiently, as it pumps more blood with each stroke and with less effort. As it pumps more blood, there is an increased capacity to eject more blood with each contraction. This occurs because the conditioned heart can hold a greater volume of blood, and when it contracts it empties more completely. Its improved ability to take in more blood is the main reason the heart often grows larger.

Along with the larger, stronger, and more efficient heart is the enlargement of existing blood vessels. They will increase in size dramatically as a result of cardiovascular conditioning. People who live sedentary lives have small arteries that are often clogged with debris, which hampers blood flow even more.

A healthy heart depends on healthy muscular tissue, and healthy muscular tissue depends on its saturation of energy-producing blood from large, healthy supply routes. This saturation, or vascularization, is one of the most important benefits of cardiovascular training. This provides the conditioned fighter with the endurance to meet the rigors of training and competing without becoming prematurely tired.

Some other benefits your body will gain from cardiovascular fitness:

1. Reduction of body fat
2. Lowering of blood pressure if originally elevated
3. Increased overall muscular strength and endurance
4. Increased functional capacity of lungs during exercise
5. Increased blood to the heart
6. Increased blood volume pumped with each heart beat

As a student of karate, you will reap many benefits applicable to your art when you increase your endurance. You will be able to increase your training time and the intensity of your workouts. Without having to pay so much attention to breathing difficulties, you'll be able to concentrate more on the intricacies of your art. This will result not only in greater enjoyment of your training, but will also result in an accelerated rate of personal progress. Also, with more oxygenated blood pumping through your body, your brain will remain alert and your reflexes will stay sharp until the end of the workout.

By contrast, fatigue will fog your thinking process and make it difficult, if not impossible, to respond either defensively or offensively during a hard sparring session or a long tournament. Your reflexes will slow or be nonexistent, and your reaction to a punch, kick, or an opening will be dangerously sluggish. Additionally, when you are tired, there is a much greater chance of accidental injury.

When your cardiovascular system is in good shape, you will find that you will be more relaxed and are able to tolerate the stress of not only a karate workout, but of daily living as well. When you are relaxed and calm, you will sleep more soundly and therefore experience greater recuperation from your hard training.

Standard solo activities considered to be good cardiovascular exercises include walking, running, jogging, swimming, and bicycling. However, some fighters find the benefits from these activities do not overlap into their karate training. In general, athletes have observed that the best way to improve heart and lung fitness for a specific activity consists of using the basic movements of the sport in question to create a cardiovascular exercise.

It is easy to adapt your solo training to a cardiovascular exercise. If you want to increase your endurance for sparring, then you should shadowbox. If you need more wind to get you through a long kata session, then you should adapt your kata training to develop lung power for that activity.

Shadowboxing is one of the best cardiovascular exercises for karate fitness.

When adapting your martial art to a cardiovascular exercise, the following requirements must be met:
1. Frequency–three to five days a week
2. Duration–fifteen to sixty minutes of continuous activity
3. Intensity–60 percent to 90 percent of maximum heart rate

To meet these requirements, you'll need to determine your maximum heart rate. A simple formula calls for you to take the number 220 (for men) or 226 (for women) and subtract your age. The difference is your maximum heart rate. Multiplying the maximum heart rate by a percentage with which you are comfortable will give you the rate to maintain while working out.

A twenty-year-old male, for example, would determine his heart rate in the following manner:

$$
\begin{array}{ll}
& 220 \text{ male} \\
\text{Subtract:} & \underline{20} \text{ age} \\
& 200 \text{ maximum heart rate} \\
\text{Multiply:} & \underline{.60} \text{ percent of maximum heart rate} \\
\text{Total:} & 120 \text{ beats per minute}
\end{array}
$$

If this male has not practiced any cardiovascular exercises for awhile, he should begin his training at 60 percent (or even 50 percent if he is in poor condition). At his chosen 60 percent, he must elevate his heartbeats to 120 per minute and maintain this level for at least fifteen minutes. As his physical condition improves, he can either exercise for a longer period of time at 60 percent or increase the intensity of his workout by moving to 70 or 80 percent of his maximum heart rate. It is not recommended that you train in the 90 percent range because of the possibility of overexertion, fatigue, and injury.

Also, it is important not to increase the intensity too soon. You want your heart and lungs to work but not at an all-out effort. Be comfortable and you will progress at a good rate.

If you want to make your shadowboxing into a cardio-vascular exercise, you will at first have to experiment to determine the intensity of movements needed to maintain your chosen maximum heart-rate percentage. Initially, you may have to check your pulse two or three times while you are solo sparring to establish your pace.

This is done by simply taking your pulse for only six seconds and immediately resuming your sparring. Mentally multiply by ten and you have your per minute reading. If your pulse reads 12 beats during your six-second check, multiplying that by ten yields 120 beats per minute. If you are a twenty-year-old male working at 60 percent, you are right on target. If your pulse is too slow, pick up the pace; if it is too fast, slow down the pace.

If you are practicing kata, take your pulse immediately upon completing the form. If your pulse is too fast or too slow, adjust the pace as you perform it again. Remember to pause no longer that six seconds between each kata. If it takes you two minutes to perform the kata, you will need to go through it ten times to receive a good 20-minute cardiovas-cular workout. Not only will your heart and lungs become stronger, but imagine how your overall kata will improve.

Working on the heavy bag is another exercise that is easily adaptable to fit cardiovascular training requirements. The tendency with bag work is for your heartbeat to elevate to a very high rate. You will have to carefully monitor it by paus-ing every so often for a six-second pulse check and make the necessary adjustment in your pace to maintain the per-centage you want.

Repetition drills are probably the easiest exercise to do to maintain your intensity level. Also, repetition drills provide you with the greatest variety of things to do during your time period. Check the chapter on reps for ideas and adapt them for endurance training.

You can combine two or more of the above exercises to provide greater variety for your cardiovascular workout.

An example of a variety-filled workout would be as follows:

Exercise	Minutes
Kata (3 times)	6
Shadowboxing	10
Rep drill	9
Total Time:	25

Whether you combine exercises or just work on one, the key is to make the solo training interesting and productive.

You will have to experiment to determine the best site to take your pulse, since one may be more prominent than another. The best locations are just below the base of the thumb on the wrist, or on the throat above the collar line and to the right or left of the windpipe. Remember to press with your fingertips, not your thumb.

Taking your pulse for longer than six seconds during the pause in activity will not yield an accurate heart rate, since the heart rapidly slows when the exercise has stopped. In fact, the faster it slows, the fitter you are. Once you catch on to how to pace yourself, you will instinctively know how fast to go. When you have achieved this level, you can just take a reading when your workout is over to ensure you were on the mark.

The real beauty of cardiovascular training is that it is easy to incorporate into your solo workouts. It never gets boring because today you might do bag work, the next workout you may decide to combine shadowboxing with reps, and the following time you may want to jog for a complete change of pace. Variety is easy with cardiovascular training. The bonus is that while your endurance improves, your sparring gets better, your power increases on the bag, and your kata becomes sharper.

Endurance fitness should be an integral part of your basic karate training. Just as your technique is important, so is the condition of your heart, lungs, and blood vessels. With a little planning, you can improve your karate and your overall physical condition.

The carotid pulse is located above the collar and to the right or left of the windpipe (left). The radial pulse is located below the base of the thumb on the wrist (right).

Chapter 6
Weight Training

There is a marked difference between karate students who lift weights and those who do not. Those who do, possess karate techniques that are stronger, faster, and more explosive. In addition, if they have followed the method described in this chapter, they will have developed greater endurance.

This is a far cry from just a few years ago when it was thought that weight training would have an adverse effect on karate technique. This may be true if the student has developed extraordinary muscle mass which would inhibit movement. It is safe to say, for instance, that Arnold Schwarzenegger will never move as quickly as Bruce Lee did.

However, when modern training methods are used, weight training will enhance your techniques and strengthen your cardiovascular system so that you have greater staying power for training and competing. The result will be that you are faster, more powerful, and will have greater endurance to keep on delivering those strong punches and kicks long after the non-weight-trained student has succumbed to exhaustion.

A standard bodybuilding routine does very little to strengthen the heart and lungs. However, when the routine has been systematically modified to meet the requirements of a cardiovascular exercise, the result is a weight-training method that develops muscular strength and also conditions the heart and lungs. In fact, there is a circular benefit to this method: as your strength increases, your endurance becomes greater, and as your endurance improves, your strength will grow.

The following exercise routine is not designed for developing a bodybuilder's physique. Although you can develop an improved muscular structure from the exercises, your objective is to increase your endurance and the power and speed of your punches, kicks, and blocks.

There is a specific sequence to the exercises, so that the heart rate is elevated and stays elevated throughout the workout. Exercises that work large muscle groups, such as the legs, will stimulate the heart rate more than exercises for the smaller muscles, such as the arms. Abdominal muscles, although small, will stimulate the heart when exercised because of the upper and lower body movement necessary to work them.

The following routine is structured so that the exercises are interspersed in such a way that the heart rate is maintained at an elevated level.

Body Part	Exercises	Reps
Abdominals	Crunches	1 set, 20 reps
Chest	Bench press	1 set, 10 reps
Abdominals	Crunches	1 set, 20 reps
Triceps (back of arms)	Press downs	1 set, 10 reps
Abdominals	Crunches	1 set, 20 reps
Back	Rowing	1 set, 10 reps
Abdominals	Crunches	1 set, 20 reps
Biceps (front of arms)	Curls	1 set, 8 reps
Abdominals	Crunches	1 set, 20 reps
Shoulders	Lateral raises	1 set, 8 reps
Abdominals	Crunches	1 set, 20 reps
Legs (front)	Leg extensions	1 set, 15 reps
Legs (back)	Leg curls	1 set, 10 reps

The bench press will develop the arms, shoulders, and chest, which are the primary muscles involved in punching and blocking. Breathe out as you press the bar up (left). Do not lock your elbows at the top (right), and breathe in as you lower the bar.

Press downs will strengthen the muscles on the back of the arms and around the elbows, which will add power to your punches and backfists. Begin with your forearms horizontal to the floor (left). Press down (right), then return to the horizontal position.

Rowing will develop the back muscles needed for powerful punching and kicking. Begin with your arm extended (left), raise the dumbbell to your armpit (right), and slowly lower it.

Alternating dumbbell curls will develop the front, upper arm muscles, used for roundhouse and uppercut punches. Slowly curl the left dumbbell (left), lower it, and then curl the right one .

Alternating lateral raises will develop the shoulder muscles that are used for the backfist and hard blocking. Raise the right dumbbell shoulder height (right), lower, and then raise the left one.

Leg extensions will strengthen the muscles around the knees to not only reinforce the joint, but to increase the power of your kicks. Start with the legs in the lowered position and then slowly raise them (left). *Do not lock the knees* in the extended position. Hold for five seconds, then lower.

Leg curls will develop the backs of the legs, which will increase the power of your kicking retraction and hook kicks. Curl the legs up toward your buttocks, hold for five seconds, then lower (right).

A hard, strong midsection will add power and explosiveness to all karate techniques. Raise your knees to your chest, cross your feet, and cross your arms behind your head (left). Keeping your chin pointing up, curl your upper body up about twelve inches (right), then lower. Experiment with different feet positions each set.

You will perform all thirteen exercises nonstop. That's right, *nonstop*. You will not rest between sets but go from one to the other until you have completed the last exercise. When you have successfully completed all thirteen exercises, you will have taken one trip through the routine. After the last exercise, rest for fifteen seconds and then take a second trip through. One trip will take at least five minutes.

For the first two or three weeks, you will probably find that three trips are plenty. You many even find that you feel a little nausea after only two trips. The routine is definitely a tough one and takes some getting used to, especially if your muscles and cardiovascular system are out of shape.

If you are trying this routine after having exercised with weights previously, you will immediately notice a decrease in the amount of weight you lift. This is because you are moving from one exercise to the next without rest. With most routines, you rest thirty to sixty seconds between sets, which allows your muscles to quickly regain their strength. In this routine, your muscles get little time to recuperate because you are working hard to keep your heart rate elevated. However, as your muscular strength and cardiovascular fitness improve, you will find your poundages begin to go back up.

Working up to a total of five trips is plenty, although you will have weak days when three trips is your maximum and there will be strong days when you want to push for a herculean seven times through.

This routine should be performed two or three times a week with at least one day of rest in between. If you are performing other cardiovascular exercises mentioned in this book, twice a week is plenty. Perform three trips for a light day and five trips through for a heavy day. Try a maximum push of six or seven trips only one day a month.

Before you begin the routine, warm up by doing push-ups, weightless squats, neck rotations, side bends, and arm rotations. The first time through, use about two-thirds of the weight you would normally use. Do this in order to warm and prepare your muscles for the next few heavier trips.

Choose a weight that makes you work hard on the last two reps without cheating. Perform the reps slowly and concentrate on the muscles being worked. On the last trip through, you may need to reduce the amount of weight of the exercises in order to get in the required reps.

Although the routine is tough, you will reap benefits in a very short time. The abdominal exercises are especially hard but will flatten and muscularize your midsection like no others. Within a very short time, you will notice your body harden, your techniques become stronger, and your endurance increase dramatically.

Chapter 7

Bag Work

The first time you punched or kicked a heavy bag, you were probably surprised, if not red-faced with embarrassment. All along you had thought your fists were dangerous weapons, and then you had to ruin your illusion by hitting the bag and discovering you had nothing more than large marshmallows sticking out of your sleeves. Yes, the bag does hit back, but with reality, not fists.

Thumb through any martial arts catalog and you will see all sizes and shapes of training devices to punch and kick. Most of them are quite good and perhaps you use some of them in your school with the aid of a training partner. When training alone, however, the most beneficial and versatile device is the old standby: the free-swinging heavy bag.

The following is just a partial list of benefits from training on the heavy bag: developing correct form; developing intensity of effort; increasing power; developing footwork; and improving endurance.

DEVELOPING CORRECT FORM

Just when you think you have the correct form to a technique, you try it on the bag and find you have to modify your delivery. It's one thing to punch and kick the air and quite

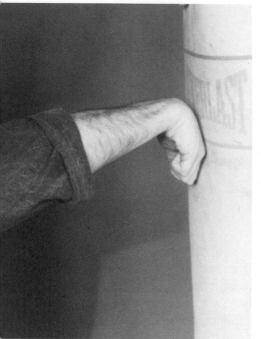 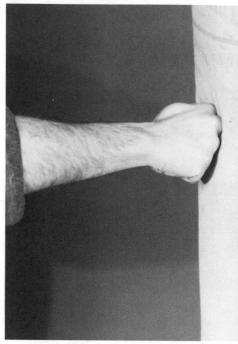

The bag has a way of informing you that your form is incorrect (left). This hurts! At first, you may want to rotate your punch only three-fourths of the way over (right). You will discover your wrist is much stronger in this position and will not buckle.

another to slam an improperly delivered foot or fist into an eighty-pound canvas bag. For example, if your spinning back kick is performed incorrectly, your foot will either slide off the bag or miss it completely. The bag definitely forces you to be accurate or you will be rewarded with pain or an injured joint.

Even though you have developed good speed in the air, you should start off hitting the bag easily in order to analyze your form and ensure that you are punching and kicking correctly. Once your techniques are landing with good form, gradually increase your speed and power until you are hitting as hard and fast as you can with accuracy and without injury.

Bag Work

DEVELOPING INTENSITY OF EFFORT

The dictionary defines *intensity* as "great energy or vehemence of emotion, thought or activity." *Vehemence* is defined as ". . . moving with great force; violent. . . ." Intensity of effort is what you want to bring to your bag workout.

The energy and vehemence with which you smash into the bag will come deep from within your mind; your muscles are conduits of this mental force. To bring it forth, you must reach into yourself and find the emotion, rage, and violence even if you are an ultra-pacifist and have never even swatted a fly. Believe that there is great violence deep within you because it is definitely there. It is a by-product of living.

An actor needing to cry before the cameras will often draw on sad personal experience and then build on it in order to get the tears flowing. You can use the same technique to bring out the emotional intensity you want to convert into energy for your bag work. Think of an experience you've had recently that stirred anger in the pit of your stomach. How about the guy who cut you off on the freeway, or the two punks who crowded in the movie line, or the drunk motorist who tossed the beer bottle on your driveway?

Although internal restraints prevent you from physically lashing out at these people, the anger is still within you. This emotion, subconsciously, builds with each negative emotional experience you have throughout the day, week, month, and year. Dig deep for it, bring it to the surface, and channel it into your techniques.

See the bag as if it were a person or experience that has filled you with anger, and take advantage of the opportunity to strike out in a way that is acceptable and healthy. You are full of anger, but the emotion is controlled and used to employ your techniques with great force.

INCREASING POWER

Hitting the bag with power does not necessarily require

101

large muscles. There are, in fact, many small karate students who can hit with such force as to virtually tear the bag off its swivel. This type of force comes from proper form, great intensity, and a coordination of well-developed muscles.

Below is a heavy bag routine that is a good basic power developer:

Technique	Reps
Front kick	15 reps each leg
Back kick	15 reps each leg
Side kick	15 reps each leg
Roundhouse kick	15 reps each leg
Reverse punch	20 reps each hand
Backfist	20 reps each hand
Round elbow	20 reps each elbow

Go completely through this power-developing routine, rest for a moment, and then go through it again. How many times you practice the routine depends upon your strength, endurance, and desire. After you have completed the basic power routine, practice a variety of combinations on the heavy bag.

Either practice your own routine or try these combinations to develop power in throwing multiple attacks.

Technique
Lead backfist, reverse punch
Lead jab, reverse punch
Reverse punch, straight punch
Reverse punch, round elbow
Lead backfist, spinning backfist
Roundhouse kick, turning back kick
Side kick, turning back kick
Double lead-leg roundhouse
Backfist, turning back kick
Reverse punch, front kick

These are not fancy, frilly techniques, but basic movements that will build power in your legs, hips, waist, chest, shoulders, and arms. If you perform ten or twenty reps per combination at least twice a week, you will quickly discover that you are hitting the bag with good, solid power.

DEVELOPING FOOTWORK

A free-swinging heavy bag allows you to move about as if you were training with a partner. You can actually spar with the bag, practicing your footwork as you shuffle, dodge, duck, and throw techniques. Shove the bag away, and as it swings back at you, throw a backfist, reverse punch combination. Move around and as the bag swings toward you again, hit it with a hard roundhouse kick. Quickly duck out of its way and hit it with elbows and knees.

An enjoyable way to work on footwork is to first punch or push the bag away (left), then sidestep and lean away as it swings back (right).

This is an excellent opportunity to work on your footwork and evasion moves. If you cannot move well, then your punches and kicks will be less effective. The free-swinging bag is a good training tool because it forces you to move, evade, and give chase while trying to hit it with maximum force.

Timing and distancing are of utmost importance. As the bag is swinging toward you, you must know exactly when to strike, because if you are too early, you will either miss or connect with a weak technique. If you hit too late and the bag is right on you, your technique will be jammed. Your footwork is critical when the bag is swinging away, because you must catch up to it and connect solidly before it swings too far out of range.

It will take you a while to consistently hit a moving bag with hard blows. But as your footwork, timing and judgment of distance improves, you will soon be punching and kicking with more and more force. You will find that you are able to quickly switch techniques, depending on where the bag is and what it is doing.

Say, for example, that you are getting ready to punch the bag as it is moving away. Just as you begin your technique, you realize the bag has swung too far for your arm to reach. Without any hesitation you throw a longer-range weapon, a front kick, which lands solidly. Or, as the bag is rushing toward you, you realize it's too close for your punch and so you switch to a close-range technique—an elbow strike.

You will find that your solo training on a free-swinging heavy bag will help when you spar. You will move about with greater confidence and have a better sense of landing solid blows on a moving target.

IMPROVING ENDURANCE

See Chapter Five for requirements of a cardiovascular exercise.

Working on the heavy bag is an excellent cardiovascular

The heavy bag will help your timing and your ability to suddenly change techniques. As you start to throw a left jab, you find the bag is moving toward you so quickly that it would be jammed (left). Instead, you quickly rotate your body and slam a close-range technique, an elbow, into the bag (right).

exercise. You are moving around quickly, bobbing, weaving, and pummeling the bag with your hands and feet; within a very short time you are sweating, breathing hard, and have an elevated heart rate. When this activity is carried out for at least fifteen minutes, you will have a good endurance-building exercise.

It doesn't matter how you train on the bag as long as you work constantly in order to maintain an elevated heart rate. You can move around the bag shadowboxing, or you can use the listed basic power drill and work the techniques repetitiously. You can use one method for the entire time period or you might mix them: shadowbox for ten minutes and do a set each from the basic power drill for another ten minutes.

The double end bag is another piece of equipment that you can use solo. This is a circular bag with elastic cords that connect to the ceiling and to the floor, and when the bag is punched it moves about erratically. Continuous practice on the bag will develop hand/eye coordination which will benefit you in hitting a small moving target, such as a head.

Chapter 8
The Final Punch

Solo training is an invaluable training experience that is missed by many martial artists. This is unfortunate, because by convincing themselves that they cannot work out alone, the students are being deprived of training that is beneficial physically, spiritually, and mentally.

In the early months of 1972, I was training hard in preparation for an advanced-degree black belt examination. The exam was a few months away and I was spending a great deal of time practicing with my classmates. However, one day a phone call informed me that I had been accepted for a much-awaited job. The call was received with mixed feelings, because the job required eighteen weeks of schooling, all of which was to take place during my usual karate classes. Since my workout partners had to work during my free time, I was suddenly thrust into a situation where I had to train alone.

For eighteen weeks, I trained by myself. Although solo training wasn't new to me, I was concerned about the impending test and my inability to train with a partner. Not being able to do anything about it, I decided to make my solo training the best I could. Most of the time, my desire to be promoted was the only motivation I needed to keep on training. Other times, on those rainy, grey days when I didn't feel quite right, I needed the variety of methods taught in this book to keep me enthused.

I trained like a crazy man. At the end of the eighteen weeks, I was in incredible shape. I had improved my endurance, speed, strength, fluidity, and fighting spirit. The many weeks of pushing and driving myself through a variety of solo-training methods had given me a stronger body and a much greater inner strength. Interestingly, I discovered I no longer *needed* these solo-training methods to get me through a workout. I used them simply because they were enjoyable and they helped me progress.

After I had resumed training in the dojo, I found that my timing was off a little since I had not trained with an opponent in four months. However, it returned quickly, just in time for the two-day testing ordeal. Although it was a tough, grueling exam, as exhausting mentally as it was physically, I had already gone through months of hard training by myself. My mind and body had been conditioned and disciplined to accept any rigorous demands.

I passed the rank test, but even more importantly, I grew as a martial artist.